Letters to 13 Berkeley Square 1841 - 1847

from W. W. Hope Esq. of Rushton Hall, Northamptonshire

By David Palmer

ACKNOWLEDGEMENTS.

I wish to thank for their help with the production of this book and supplying some of the photographs and illustrations:

John Bazin (Elegant Carriages)
Violet Caillebotte
Country Life Magazine
Rod Davis
Tom and Valerie Hazelton
Peter Hill
David and Heather Pain
Joan Palmer
Sarah Palmer
Gladys and the late George Dainty

David Palmer

ISBN No: 978-0-9554981-0-7

Published by David Palmer

Printed by: Phoenix Printing Company, Rothwell, Northamptonshire

Introduction

In a chance meeting with someone in Rushton village hall, the conversation came round to village history and Rushton Hall. They said that there were "just some old note books kept by the bailiff at the hall in the 1840's, they were not very interesting and were hard to read", but I asked if I could see them, and borrow them to read. I was expecting the type of note book that bailiffs, farmers and tradesmen carry in their pockets to make notes in, but much to my surprise and delight they were nothing of the sort.

The two books were nine inches by fourteen inches bound in leather. They contained about three hundred pages of copies of every letter sent out from Rushton Hall and there were copies of letters that Mr Hope had sent to Rushton Hall from Paris. Some letters were in perfect writing in the hand of Mr Brunning the Bailiff or a clerk. Other letters are sent from Paris by Mr Hope and are also easy to read as they are in a clerk's hand, though some are in the hand of Mr Hope, and some in French by a clerk.

All are a delight to read and give an insight to the side of Victorian life in a style I have never seen before.

The books have been copied out in two parts:

> Part one - Letters from Mr Hope to Rushton Hall - *Contained in this book, this includes a catalogue for the auction of the contents of Rushton hall after the death of W. W. Hope in 1855*
>
> Part two - Letters to Mr Hope from Rushton Hall. (in a book to follow)

All the letters had to go via Mr Hope's agent Mr V. Crosby at the London house that Mr Hope had, at 13 Berkeley Square.

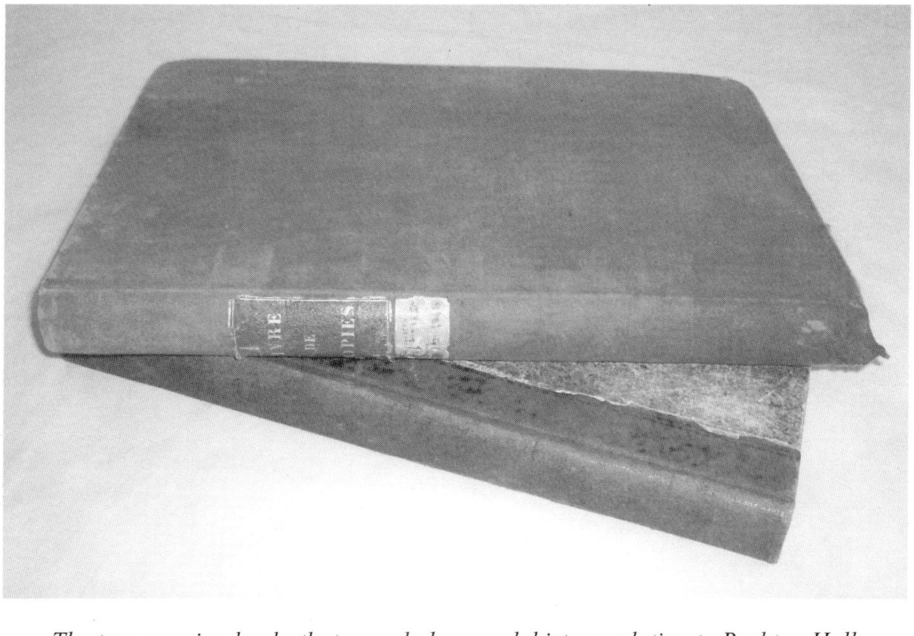

The two amazing books that revealed so much history relating to Rushton Hall

A Guide to Rushton Hall Estate

The magnificent Rushton Hall was built in local Weldon limestone during the late sixteenth and seventeenth century, by Sir John Tresham and enlarged by his son Sir Thomas Tresham.

The building was confiscated by the Crown from the Treshams due to their connections with the Gun Powder Plot.

The estate was then bought by Sir William Cockayne in 1619.

In 1828 the estate was sold to William Williams Hope of Paris. A partner in the banking company of Hope & Co of Amsterdam. He bought the estate for £140,000.

Mr Hope rebuilt most of the Hall and added a new kitchen and stables, almost every house in the village was rebuilt and he also built a new Public House, called 'The Hope Arms'. A new school and school house were added for the village, plus several new farm houses and farm buildings, along with the planting of new woodlands.
The two lodge gate houses of the hall were removed and rebuilt in their present position. All we see today we have to thank Mr Hope for, along with his main architect and steward of Rushton Hall, Mr John Brunning.

Mr Hope died in Paris in January 1855 and his executors sold the estate to the Clerke - Thornhill family for £165,000. In August 1855 all the furniture and all the contents owned by Hope were sold in an auction sale that lasted ten days.
In Mr Hopes will he left most of his money to ladies of Paris.

In 1931 the estate was sold to Mr G. Pain & Mr. D. W. Pain, they never resided in the hall. The army used the hall during the second world war.
The hall then stood empty until 1957 when it was purchased by the Ministry of Work. It was converted in to a school for the Royal National Institute for the Blind.

In 2004 the Hall and grounds were sold on and have been converted into a grand hotel and restaurant.

All the houses in the village have been sold over the years to private owners, as have the farms and woodlands.

Sir Thomas Tresham

Preface

William Williams Hope, was born in 1802 in Amsterdam; his father John Williams added the name Hope to him when he married his partners' niece. The company where John Williams worked was Hope & Co Bankers.

Williams father died when he was eleven, leaving him with a vast amount of money, he inherited a large estate in Cornwall, which included some mines. At the age of twenty six, William bought Rushton estate, which included a grand hall, the village and four thousand acres. The hall was in need of repairs, and then there was a fire at the hall in 1836.
One day Mr Hope was coming out of a London theatre and saw a duel taking place, outside, Hope got talking to one of the dualists a Mr John Brunning. It is said that it was the last duel fought in London.

Mr Brunning and Mr Hope got talking and Hope discovered that Brunning was just the man he needed to rebuild Rushton Hall, he was a master builder. John Brunning, his wife and niece then came from Suffolk to live at Rushton Hall and rebuild it. Most of what we today was built or rebuilt by Brunning.

Mr Hope had a grand house at number 13 Berkeley Square, London, where his agent for his estates lived - Mr V. H. Crosby. William Williams Hope seldom came to England, but when he did, he had a short stay in London, and then went on to Rushton which he loved, as it reminded him of where he lived as a child. Most of his life he lived at 121 Rue Dominique, Fabourg St Germaine, Paris.

He kept a copy of every single letter he or his clerk sent for him in a large green suede leather bound copy book, with 'Livre de copies' most in gold and red lettering on the backing. This book contains about seven hundred and eighty letters, both business and private letters were recorded in the book.
Many of the letters were written in French, some not much more tha note to the bank asking for more money or to a local tradesman.

Most of the letters he sends to Rushton Hall tell of his life, the time and transport of the 1840's. This book contains copies of the most interesting letters in the book. It also contains a copy of the sales catalogue of the contents of Rushton Hall in 1855 after the death of W. W. Hope.

The auction lasted ten days and was one of the largest auctions ever held in Northamptonshire.

The photographs and illustrations in this book are scenes that Mr Hope would have been familiar with, but they are not all true to the period of his ownership.

All letters written on behalf of W.W. Hope are printed in italics.

A brief history of 13 Berkeley Square

Number 13 Berkeley Square has had some interesting owners, the first being a Mr Edward Bouverie, who planted Plane trees in the square opposite his house.

The next owner was Dutch, born 1802 - 1855 Mr William Williams Hope of Paris who never lived there but kept his estate manager Vinus Hodgekinson Crosby there to run his English properties.

When Hope died in 1855 the house was owned by Admiral Rouse who at one time was Director of the Jockey Club.

Then the property came into the hands of the Marquis of Hertford, next came the famous Lord Carnarvon from 1900 -1910 the finder of the Tomb of Tutankhamen.

Since then Number 13 has been rebuilt many times. The only thing that remains the same is the square.

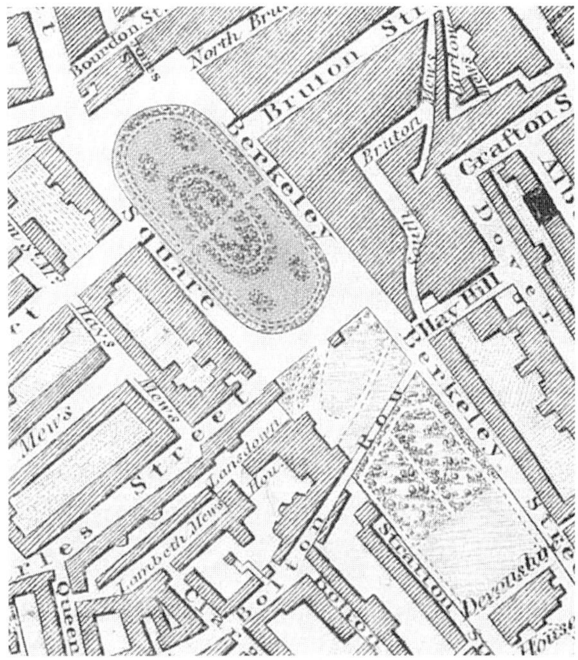

Mr. Hope's House in Paris is now the Hotel De Monaco and the Polish Embassy.

Information about some of the characters in this book

1. **Mr William Williams Hope**. Born Amsterdam 1802, he was the son of a very wealthy banker. He owned land in Leicestershire, Cornwall, Northamptonshire, and France, plus a grand house in both London and Paris.
2. **Mr. Vinus Hodgekinson Crosby**. Born 1795 in London, he was an accountant and agent in full charge of all Mr. Hopes estates.
3. **Mrs Hannah Crosby**. Born Sussex 1810, she married V. H. Crosby in 1844. They lived in Mr Hopes London house. Mrs Crosby had the nickname Fiffey. She was in charge of all Mr Hopes household when he came to England and when he stayed at Rushton Hall.
4. **Mr. John Brunning** Born in Suffolk in 1790 and in 1835 he came to Rushton to be in charge of the rebuilding of the Hall. In 1844 he became agent in charge of all Mr Hopes properties in England. When he retired, he built a small but grand house on the edge of Rothwell called Suffolk Villa.
5. **Mrs Matha Brunning**. Born in Suffolk in 1804 she was the wife of John Brunning and they had no children. Mrs Brunning was in charge of the poultry and the dairy at the Hall and their accounts.
6. **Miss Nantz Dunn** the sister of Mrs Crosby and the house keeper to Mr & Mrs Crosby.
7. **Mr Birmingham** Mr Crosby's servant.
8. **Mr Hooper** a coach builder of Haymarket, London.
9. **Mr Thomas Puckford** in charge of lands and mines in Cornwall, he had the title of Captain as was given to all Cornish Mine Managers
10. **Mr Whiteley** the agent in Cornwall for Mr Hope.
11. **Mr William Moffat** estate manager at Rushton before Mr Brunning.
12. **Mr Watkinson** the farm bailiff at Rushton
13. **Mr John Cobley** the groom at Rushton Hall.

Glossary

Avelines - A type of nut
Barouche - A four wheeled carriage that seats four with a let down hood.
Brake or Break - A small wagon for light work with four wheels
Captain - A Cornish Mine Manager
Chariot - A four wheeled carriage with back seats only.
Dilligence - A public stage coach used in France.
Dog Cart - A two wheeled light horse cart, common for ladies to drive.
Fly - A light one horse carriage with two wheels.
Jacks - Pike (fish)
Set - A Cornish mine.
Spring Cart - A light, two large wheeled horse drawn cart.
Store - Animals bought to grow on.
Trap - A two wheeled very light driving cart.
Tub - A small horse cart that was light and round for taking children about in.
Village itch - Scabies or skin mites.
Wafer (wafering in black) - A type of sealing wax that can be removed.

Contents

Chapter One

October 1841 to December 1841

A Barouche Carriage

V. Crosby Esq. **Minnil 16th October 1841**

My dear Crosby,

I did not say that Moffat was displeased with Brunning, but I am, so I think he could have finished everything at Rushton before now.

Hannah's system of beer will do very well in London, but I cannot answer in the country, as besides the regular beer wanted, there are daily twenty different people that come from a distance, such as workmen, neighbours, servants, trades people etc. to whom you must give beer. If you did not, you would get a very bad name and one could not have a person running down every morning to the public house in the village to get a glass of ale. It is on that account a foreigner will not do as he would not know how to distribute it, and he must be an Englishman; a man you can depend on. You see how necessary a house steward will be to me after all.

There are a few kitchen utensils wanted at Rushton, which cannot be got in London, but will the customs house in London admit them? The last time I sent some clocks, some formality had been forgotten, which almost prevented them getting in. Will you enquire what it is, and what forms we need, as I shall want to send a large clock and four candelabras over to England for Rushton? Though last, not least, will you enquire if I can get three bonnets and some gowns through customs if they are half made up? I have some ornamental sashes and petticoats, everything prepared, so that I could easily have them made up. Was it a very good plan that I shall send all these things by Louis the courier? These are my offerings to the young ladies.

What terrible weather, I hope it will be over before the time I start. I hope to be in London on Monday the 8th of November. My servants will arrive some time before.

Has Moffat received my letter? I wrote to him about Mrs Clarke, directly in answer that his predecessor chose not to listen to Mrs Clark's vagaries and used to wait till the storm had blown over. It seems that he has acted by my advice and he says that Mrs Clarke is now quite civil. This is very well for the time being, but I have made up my mind to dismiss her as soon as I can replace her.

Pray will you enquire for a good fashionable tailor in London? I am so disgusted with French tailors and French cloth that I intend having some clothing made in England.

You must take out a shooting licence. Tell Hannah to put it down in her book. As soon as Hannah can, she must get Brunning and Nantz to make a regular inventory of the whole of the house of everything. My next letter will be to Hannah containing a list of everything wanted at London and Rushton.

I also have written a letter to Brunning that he must see if he can find the chests that were made some years ago, wherewith he will send things from London to Rushton. They were made so that when empty they would fit inside one another. Also, double keys were made; one set for London the others for Rushton. I have told Brunning to look for these chests, repair them, complete them and deliver them to Hannah. They will do very well for the things that have to go to Rushton. These chests must be numbered and Hannah must keep a note in a book of when they are sent to Rushton and when they come back. This must be done every time. I shall repeat my litany over again: I wish to have a steward who would save me doing all this writing.

My Love to the young ladies, believe me, Mr W. W. Hope.

P. S. See in your letter to Hannah that you only give a pint a man now at Rushton. It has always been the custom and I believe in all English houses to give the servants as much table beers as they like besides a pint per meal, as the English servants like their ales. English Gentlemen like their wine after dinner.
On second thoughts, I think the reason Mrs Clarke went sulky must have been Brunnings fault. He most likely dislikes the house, nothing finished, things everywhere and workmen making a mess. Nantz complains about similar things.

Send me a starting time list for Ostend to London for this Month.
Believe me

W. W. Hope

Mr Crosby **Paris 19th October 1841**

My dear Crosby,

Next week Louis will arrive in London with two horses, and a box containing papers, another with kitchen utensils, and one with a clock in it and another with four candelabras. All this is to go direct to Rushton. Also, there will be two boxes containing things for the ladies of which I beg their acceptance.

I will write to Moffat to send a man to London to collect the two horses. I expect Louis will get to Boulogne on the 26th or 27th and that he shall call at my house at No 13 Berkeley Square, that you may give him some directions where he is to go with the horses. I have told Louis to put them up at the first livery stables, or you could give him Mr Ivan's address. I could tell him that if you could send me Mr Ivan's address, Louis could then go there. Do you think Brunning should meet him to help him get all things clear through the customs house? I expect Louis will start by the Boulogne boat on Tuesday the boat at six in the morning, therefore, we can calculate when he arrives.

In your walks about London see if you can find about a small travelling chariot, which can be used at my town house, but there must be a boy on the front to drive it. This I believe will be the best thing; it could be very useful.

Your friend Baron Roger has died.

There is a dancer in Paris that will delight you.

Believe me, W. W. Hope.

M de Morel ***14 Rue Nr des Mathurins 24th October 1841***

My dear Sir,

I feel that it would be a good idea to delay selling everything that we have in stock until the news is better. If this does not work, on my return we could sell at a higher price in order to reduce any losses. Thereafter, if this should fail, we will buy to cover our losses.

Next Thursday at one o'clock, I will be at home in Paris. Thank you for all your letters.
Do not write to me Tuesday in the country, that for Thursday please send to Paris.

Best wishes etc.

M. Martins ***24th October 1841***

Jean,

I found the following items on a list of things to bring back to Rushton.

Lampshades
Mint Essence
Salad dish
Something to uncork champagne.
Please bring anything you cannot buy in London back with you from Paris. Bring all of it, or put it in my coach. I think that it would be better to buy all of it in Paris.
I will return to Paris very early on Thursday morning. There are not any orders for the messenger. I hope he can be useful in the country. Just send a coach to Paris. Put the enclosed letters through the door at our place.

Regards.

Mr Moffat ***24th October 1841***

NOTE FOR LONDON

- *2lbs semolina*
- *25lbs Of grey salt*
- *25lbs Of white malt*
- *6 blocks of sugars*
- *12-15 francs per block 8lbs of Italian macaroni*
- *12lbs of Carolina Rice*
- *2lbs of pearl barley*
- *20lbs of Malaga grapes*
- *20lbs of Corinthian grapes*
- *10lbs of Smyman grapes without pips*
- *1lb of crystallized oranges 1lb of white pepper*
- *12 muscadets*
- *½ lb of mignonette*
- *1 of cloves*
- *1 small flagon of carmine*
- *½ lb of sago*
- *1lb of potato flakes*
- *12lbs of quality oil*
- *3 bottles of ordinary oil*
- *1 Bottle of vinegar*
- *2 bottles of tarragon vinegar*
- *1 jar of anchovies*
- *1 pot of gherkins*
- *100 lemons*
- *½ lbs of green coffee*
- *4lbs of parmesan cheese*
- *1lbs of tea*
- *4 pots of ground mustard*
- *1 pot of ordinary mustard*
- *1 cake of cafsonade*
- *1 flagon of prowder' pepper*
- *1 flagon of anchovy essence*
- *1 pot of capers*
- *1 flagon of Turkish Wheat*
- *1 small cask of black soap*
- *4lbs of white soap*
- *1 bottle of ink*
- *1 packet of pens*
- *1 ream of office paper*
- *12 books of letter paper*
- *2 hands of filter paper*
- *1 quart of vanilla*
- *1/4 of angelica*
- *½ lb of fish glue*

- *6lbs of sweet almonds*
- *1/4 of orange flower pralines*
- *2lbs of vanilla chocolate*
- *1 bottle of orange flower water*
- *½ lb of pistachios*
- *12 reels of thread*
- *6 of phosphor lighters*
- *1 bottle of Spanish white*
- *5lbs of Tea for the office*
- *5lbs of Coffee for the office*
- *20lbs of sugar for the office*
- *3lbs of Tea for Mr Hope*
- *4lbs of chicken stock*
- *6 bottles of rum fruit preserves*
- *4 bottles of red currant juice jam*
- *6 pots of apricot marmalade*
- *6 pots raspberry and red currant jelly*
- *18lbs of bar red currants*
- *6 pots of cherries*
- *6 hams*
- *2 etamines*

REMINDER
I need to buy some lard when Mr Jean arrives so that he can explain me the necessary (? Could read "how it is made), (or how he makes it)

NOTE FOR THE OFFICE

- *8lbs of almonds*
- *½ lbs of almonds*
- *2lbs crushed avelines*
- *50 lemons }The freshest possible*
- *20 oranges }*
- *10lbs of ground Mocha coffee from Martinique*
- *½ ream of office paper.*

Mr Crosby ***Minnil***

Mr Crosby,

John was too late for the post. I have therefore opened this letter to beg you to read the enclosed. It's to Mr Moffat. I will explain to you what I have ordered him to do with the horses.

Louis will, I think, certainly start from Boulogne on Thursday the 26th. Enclosed is a note for Brunning. Will you also enquire about the Kettering coach?

After reading Moffats letter, put it in the post and give the other letter to Brunning.

***Mr Brunning**,*

Mr Hope requests Mr Brunning will keep the key of the private staircase by him, and not deliver it to anybody else. Mr Hope requests Mr Brunning will write to him on this subject, and also to tell him if he has ordered a carpet for the front anti-room at Rushton, as he cannot recall anything about it.

Signed for W. W. H.

Mr Crosby ***Paris 22nd October 1841***

My dear Crosby,

I have determined to take Prahi with me, and make him manage the beer.

Grey breeches always last a year with my servants, give Prahi a new pair. All the servants are to have a new great coat; you can have them made directly.

I have given up on Mr Michel, but I intend having a tailor on both sides of the water so to have the best of each. I have a monstrous mind to give you the Louis XVI shooting jacket and waistcoat. They have flaps in the front and are very comfortable, tell me if you should like them? They are made of a very nice dark grey corduroy cloth in velvet.
You told me you wanted breeches for the Keeper to be made in London; they would go well together.

None of my servants smoke except the under cook and the courier. I shall strictly forbid it. You must keep up the fires in the smoking room, and when there is a fire in the room, open the bookcase door where the cigars are kept.

About your boots, John can bring you a pair. Write me a note for your boot maker by return post.

Will you ask Hannah to write to me, to tell me which is the coach by which the game and poultry are to be sent to London, and if the cheapest still runs?

I am sorry you did not write me sooner about your boots, as Louis could have taken you a pair, but as I am in Paris, he would not get my letter in time as he starts for England early tomorrow morning.

For W. W. H.

Mr Crosby ***Paris 23rd October 1841***

Dear Crosby,

In consequence of Rosemary wishing to start two days later, I shall not be in London until the 10th. This will give you plenty of time for your boots.

As you kindly offered to teach John and the two Peters how to manage the beer, order in a small cask of ale, and show them how to draw and tap it. Also, order a cask of best beer for the table and teach them the amount to give each man per meal.

I intend to stay at Rushton till the end of the month, then a few days after my departure I shall ask you and Fiffey to come to Paris until about May. Louis will bring over two boxes, one containing two hats, one for Hannah

For W. W. H.

Mr Moffat **Minnel 20th Oct**

Mr Moffat,

As soon as you secure this letter, will you take measures to send a proper person for two horses that will arrive in London on the 26th of this month? I think that unless you have someone you think better, John Cobly would be a proper person. He must be in London on that day, so ask him to call at my house No 13 Berkeley Square at 12 o clock and ask for Mr Crosby, who will tell him where the horses will be, and what time they should arrive. They will come by steam packet from Boulogne to London Bridge. They will require rest and travel gently.

You will give John Cobly or whoever you send, a letter written by you and addressed to Mr Crosby, to inform gentlemen that the bearer John Cobly is the person you have sent up to town to fetch the horses by my orders. You will tell the man how he is to travel to Rushton, whether by road or by rail road.

You will do that as you think proper, direct him accordingly and to give him the money requested for the journey.

The horses are old ones and very quiet and very practical. They have with them old saddles, horse cloths and harness for the two horses. You will direct the coachman Asher of Harborough to proceed with all dispatch with the carriage and they are to be finished and returned to Rushton by the 3rd of November at the latest.

Will you write me by return of post if there is a coach that runs from Kettering to London and visa versa, and what are the hours of starting?

Also, what is the amount of money in the Harborough bank?

Tell the gardener to have all his fruit, pears and apples arranged and sorted against my arrival.

Will you also enquire if there is a coach that runs from Kettering to the railroad and what hours? Have you got a new coachman?

I shall want in the house during my stay at Rushton, the assistance of Bamford, who was in the house when I was last at Rushton. Will you tell me if he is willing to come?

Signed for W. W. H.

Mrs Crosby **Paris 23rd October 1841**

My dear Hannah,

With this letter, I sent you a list of provisions wanted at Rushton. All those that will not spoil, you had better send directly by wagon, and let Moffat know and informed when they should arrive and that they are to be put in a dry place there.

Things that spoil had better be sent so that they are at Rushton the same time as John. All things marked with a cross are for the kitchen, those marked office are for Mr Brunning and the list marked all for Prati are for him.

Each trunk has been packed with great care and there is a list of their contents on the inside of each lid. Unpack in order; do not mix first with the last. Coming from Paris to London and on to Rushton there will be four Cooks, two Peter's, Prati and John.

If you have not a room fresh, John or Prati can go in the worse spare bedroom in the front of the house. Nantz will remain in her room; Mr Venneruy can be in his old room with another gentleman. Some other gentlemen will come along, so another bedroom will be wanted at Rushton.

Things that will be wanted are:

Two very small teapots (to make one cup of beverage: if a person is ill, a china or metal will do.
A few sticks of sealing wax and a box of black wafers.
A small bell for the dinner table.
Twelve candle sticks and snuffers, but only if you think we need them.
Twelve extinguishers like the ones you sent last year.
Some nice little oil lights, which can be carried about like a flat candlestick.
Three large sponges and a hone for sharpening penknives.
Some pencils and India rubber.

John forgot to put on the list what sort of coffee, what to roast and what sort not to.
Do not forget saltcellars. Please keep a list of what you have and tell Hannah not to forget the bottoms of the saltcellars this time.

For W. W. H.

Mr Moffat ***Paris 24th October 1841***

Dear Sir,

It is requested for you to open the new safe from time to time to air and see no damp gets in. Have you examined the wine cellars lately? If they are getting damp, let in the air so they can dry out.

Pray ask the clerk if he wants anything from London. There will be coming over from London: four cooks, two Peters and an additional servant. Tell him to prepare all the rooms and light good fires, which are to be kept up everywhere. He had better get an additional woman for the kitchen, Hefford or Bamford or anybody else wishes of the letter she may like.

Mr Bamford is to have a new suit of livery. A grey coat of plantation yellow and one of canary yellow colour with dark green or black plush breeches. The buttons white and silvered, quite plain, nothing on them except arms. Have them engraved for the keeper; they might be white or plain. He must also have a couple of sound jackets for morning work and made of stuffs such as the indoor servants usually have. A hat with a silver edging band round it. He must also have a Red waistcoat for morning work. This livery when I leave Rushton, you will put carefully away and only use when I come again. The coachman is to have a great cravat in blue with a grey coat, yellow waistcoat. Plush breeches and matching boots; coat and hat to have a lace band on it. Also, a working drip hat and coat.

All these things are to be made by the tailor in Harborough and to be well fitted and finished before I arrive, all to be made as cheap as possible.
For W. W. H. P.S. The poultry man must begin to fatten the poultry.

W. Moffat. ***Paris 28th October 1841***

W. Moffat,

I have received your letters of the 24th & 25th. When I said you were not to keep the workman on, I meant to workmen in extraordinary. Sam Crighton and John Bull are not in that category, you will keep them on. With respect to a new coachman, I will trust you to find one. Try to get one that can read and write. He is to live at the stables with his wife, but they must conduct themselves with great propriety. What do you intend to give him for board and pay? Pray send me by return of post the exact sums of money that is in the Bank from lands etc. If there is anything the coachman might need in the stables, you had better buy it and let me know the costs.

For W. W. H.

Paris 30th October 1841
Messrs Adams & Hooper
Coach Builders
London.

Gentlemen,

I find the following defects in the carriages. By putting the hatbox underneath behind, you throw all the weight before, which will make the carriage very uneasy, I think the carriage is too low in the drawing. The front wheels will not pass underneath, so I propose to remedy the inconvenience in the following manner: let the front hooks be made, two under the carpet boxes and cases. Behind, put the trunks and over the boot behind, the ladies hat boxes.

The interior will be fitted up in Paris. I think the boot or hatbox at present are too large and they ought to be diminished. I have drawn a line; in every case, the hind boxes for trunks ought to be smaller, as when the carriage is used in town it would not look too unsightly. Springs must be made to carry a good weight.

In Germany, they have a shoe that you can put on or take off without getting out of the carriage. Take care that the seat is not too deep, but that you can sit in the seat with your hat on.

The carriage to be built immediately for the price on £120 and to be ready as soon as possible

For W. W. H.

Mrs Crosby **Paris 30th October 1841**

My dear Hannah,

Herewith I send you and Nantz a list of your things, that you may see exactly if they are the same as the list John showed me.

Yes, Cafe Vert means not roasted; all the rest is to be roasted.

Did you see the old horse while in London? I am afraid poor Savin will die, he is very old and ill, he is 23 years old.

Ever W. W. H.

V. Crosby Esq. **Paris 30th October 1841**

My dear Crosby,

I enclose a list of observations for Hooper and the order for building the carriage, the drawing, a list of ladies things and a letter for Hannah.

About coming to Paris. I can manage it for you, but I can explain that better myself than writing. Read my observations on the carriage and keep a copy.

Sincerely Ever, W. W. H.

Mr W. Moffat, *Paris November 1st 1841*

I am always expecting an answer to my letter regarding what the keeper may want.
I hope he does not want too much, as he has taken so long to answer my questions.

On Monday the 8th of November, there will arrive by the Kettering coach: Mr John Martins my head butler and three servants. The Break and a small cart must be at Kettering waiting for them, ready to convey them and their baggage to Rushton immediately you receive notice of their coming, by a note, which Mr Crosby will address to you.

On that day, you will have killed and brought into the house at Rushton:
1 Ox
1 Fat pig
2 Sheep
1 Calf and everything that belongs to the same.
6 Old hens
6 Fat fowl
1 Turkey
2 Pheasants
2 Partridges
12 Pigeons and 4 Ducks.

On the 10th, you must bring in to the house six more partridges and whatever else Mr Martins may want. You will send him the assistance in your power, as he and my other servants are foreigners and hardly speak any English.

You will also send into the kitchen for the 8th of November, one sack of flour, the finest you can get, taking care in its selection yourself.

The two horses I have sent over, you can make use of them in order to let the old horse rest and be given gentle work.

The poultry man must put up plenty of poultry. When the ox is killed, there are certain parts, which you hand over to the butcher, for which he must account to you for, such as fat, which my cook does not want. Of the calf's things, everything, I believe must be sent in. The Butcher knows what part of the fat of that was usually sold to him from my account by your predecessor. If you do not have a pig, you must buy one for him. The ox and sheep are to be the best you can pick out on your own. The Keeper will kill the game. There was a Custom at Rushton that must be put to end, which was this; There is a great quantity of refuse meat, which having been boiled is no more use in the house and in the past given to the poor, they were in the habit of coming to fetch it at the Hall . This is no more to be done, as it opens the door for robbery. So you must have it properly distributed among the poor that are deserving, from your house. Can you see as much as possible, to keep any strangers or people coming to see my servants? You have no doubt by this time become acquainted with Rushton and you will tell me when we shall be able to shut up those back gates entirely.

I see there is some burning in the area. You must from time to time exercise your horses and man with a fire drill, with the engine, so that on any emergency they might go the distance. The men must be drilled to this sort of work, and an engine is a very useful thing, but you have to try it every now and then.

It will be necessary that you send up to London direct to Mrs Crosby as per mail, to be left at the Bull and Mouth Coach Office in Regents Circus till called for:
3 Brace of partridges
4 Old hens
8 Fowl
4 Ducks
2 Pheasants
2 Leverets.

You will advise her on the day before as per letter of their departure. You will take note of this for future ease, as it is the cheapest was of having things sent to London. Be sure to address to Mrs Crosby's address at 13 Berkeley Square.

Signed for W. W. H.

2nd November 1841

This last order of game and poultry, you will send to London immediately on arrival of this letter. I have deferred the sending of this letter till today, as I was in hope to have received your answer to my letter of the 22nd of October. I ought to have had an answer a few days ago; this deferment will cause me some inconvenience, but I suppose the Master Keeper has done it, that he may send guns to London or have things done himself.

This I really forbid, my orders are that nothing is to be done till I come. If there is anything wanting, I shall most likely discharge him, unless he can explain himself.

I ought to have answers from yourself by this time.

Signed for W. W. H.

V. Crosby **Paris November 1st 1841**

Mr dear Crosby,

John started this morning at 10 o'clock; he will arrive tomorrow in Boulogne from whence he will precede to Dover and then London. I think you may expect him in London on Thursday the 4th, very early that morning or late evening.

The rest of the servants will start tomorrow from Boulogne, and thence directly to London, they will arrive shortly after John.

Those who come over thus are Prati and long Peter; also, four cooks. Will you be so good as to take some inside places in the coach for Kettering, which starts from London on Monday the 8th? John and Peter and the two cooks are to start by it. If you can get the places, write Moffat and note that there are four servants coming down by the day coach and that the break and a small cart must be waiting for them to convey them and their baggage to Rushton.

I want you to do this as I am not sure whether you can get places and if not, send them down in the best way that you think and in the best manner. You will have to give notice to Moffat accordingly.

I have had a letter from Louis, who has gone to Antwerp to buy some vases for me. He will be there forty-eight hours and will then meet Boudelle there and then go into Belgium and Holland to look for more vases. I have told them to buy china vases for me. It will take them five days to get from Rotterdam to my house in Paris. The answer is beautiful for what I want.

I have written to John to arrange with you and Hannah the best way I can bring with me another man like Peter and he will do the work when in London. Show Peter and his brother what jobs to do. Do not forget to show Prati the exact measures of ale per man that is given out at each meal.

I believe that Frenchmen will not drink much table beer per meal, but to the Englishmen it is customary to give table beer as they like it. This is about one pint of ale per meal.

I do not know if any more is given at supper? Hannah will no doubt tell you.

Poor old Barbajar is dead. Will you read Moffats enclosed letter and make a note of it. It will save the trouble of repeating the contents to you. Copy it and send it to him.

I did not dream it was all saints day, so my letter will miss the post.

Believe me W. W. Hope.

****This was enclosed with the last letter for Mr. Crosby****

Mrs Crosby,

My dear Hannah,

Will you keep separate accounts of everything that goes to Rushton, but be sure to keep this separate; when I say keep separate, I really mean it.

When you get to Rushton, you will ask Moffat for any money owing by showing him the account book, and he must then pay you separately for that, and he will charge it to his book,

Believe me W. W. Hope.

P.S. forward to Mr Crosby.

Yesterday I was a great deal to late for the post. The carriage arrived quite safe this morning. Go to Manton's and take five hundred cups, they will always be wanted.

You had better go the Regents Circus coach office to see if there have been any time changes, and advise Moffat so.

Did you find the stockings all right and a good fashion?

Believe me W. W. Hope.

V Crosby   Paris 11th December 1841

My dear Crosby,

On the third page, you will find observations about the new travelling carriage. I have received your letters of the 2nd and 8th. If you see Jennings, try to have him draft an agreement between Brunning and me, made as short as possible. I think that will be best.

When you come over, Birmingham tells me you will have no boating? Will you cross on a new moon or a full one? A full moon is on the 28th, so you will have to answer to the tide. Try to arrive before Christmas day in London.

Has Moffat got all the buttons you ordered? In answer to your letter, Marsh is very ill and breaking up. Beaumont says the Tories are good for nothing. None too keen on the wigs, they are no help.

Give my respects to her Ladyship.

Believe me, W. W. Hope.

P.S. Carlotta Gris is a most delightful dancer.

Tell Hooper what I think about his carriage, I do not admire the footboards to the front and behind dickey. The straight line of the boot and the curve of the footboards will make a receptacle for mud. The footboard ought not to look detached from the boot, unless it is necessary in order to remove the dickeys, which would be a good plan.

The imperials ought to be divided into six, thus the two centre ones being narrow might be made deeper. The hind bos must have several strong boxes; the front box, nothing carpetbags and other things will be stowed away there. I wish for Mr Hooper to make a new drawing on some paper with explanations. Is not the carriage rather too long? There must be a good seat box inside.

Believe me, W. W. Hope

V Crosby   Paris 14th December 1841

I am sadly in need of some vases. I have decided upon sending Bondelle. He will go by the Boulogne boat and he can be in London by Sunday evening. John's or the cooks' room will do for him.

You had better take a fly and take him around the shops, and see if Brunning cannot find out some warehouses in the city where one can buy large vases from China or Japan, old ones will do. Two days should suffice to see and buy them. Brunning will get men to pack them under his directions, and you will ship them off with the first Calais to Boulogne boat that will take all of the cases. Hannah will advance the money necessary out of what is in her hands.

When you come over, will you bring me over some presents, prints and caricatures and keepsakes to put on my table in my drawing room? Some will amuse people when they call. I shall write to you again tomorrow. Only set Brunning to work on finding those addresses.

Believe me W. W. Hope

V Crosby **Paris 15th December 1841**

My dear Crosby,

I am sorry I cannot manage things for you better, but it is impossible for me to get things ready for you so soon. Boudelle will be on Sunday evening in London by the Boulogne boat. He leaves Boulogne at three in the morning. It will perhaps be better for you only to start on the 26th. The tide will answer for you and you will be travelling on Christmas day, I think that is in two days.

Believe me W. W. Hope.

V Crosby **Paris 13th December 1841**

I had written so far yesterday when I was interrupted. As you have an objection to travelling on Christmas day, suppose you can start on the 27th and if there is no boat on the 27th then it must be the 28th.

I will send Louis and he will be waiting for you at Calais or I could send him all the way to London if you prefer it, as it would save you a great deal time at Dover. Boudelle could come as well; they could take a Fly and go around the shops. Brunning will do the packing with the help of Boudelle; the vases must be packed extra well. By sending Louis, you can come to Paris early in two days from Calais.

Tell Hannah I want some shirt buttons of the common size. Do not forget to pay off what remains at Manton's. I want some English pins and some black ones for the ladies.

Boudelle will bring with him a letter of credit for you on Messrs Harman's bank for a thousand pounds, in case the money in Hannah's hands should be spent, and more is wanted.

Bring me over the price of the clothes at the tailors, and all the charges he makes for the liveries. Tell him to write them out so that I can compare them with Paris prices. Bondelle will have a list of the things I want him to buy. Pray appraise him as much as you can. I have a monstrous deal of trouble with my establishment here at present.

Believe me W. W. Hope.

V Crosby **Paris 18th December 1841**

My dear Crosby,

Will you tear off the third page of this letter or give the letter to Boudelle that he may read what is on page three. I have given him ten sovereigns, should he want any more you must supply him.

Give my respects to her Ladyship.

You can send things by Boudelle if you wish to have room in your carriage. The Stilton cheese for example. I wish Hannah to enquire the price of stilton in London. I wish she would send some good hams and some tongues by Boudelle.

Believe me W. W. Hope.

P.S. If you do not get the letter of credit on Harman's Bank, perhaps you could take this letter and show them my signature. As soon as Boudelle has finished shopping, ship him with the vases back on the first Calais or Boulogne boat.

Mrs Crosby **Paris 22nd December 1841**

My dear Hannah,

Louis starts for England this evening. Tell Mr Crosby that if he and Boudelle find some vases they must buy them, even if they are rather dear.

I cannot write to you much longer as I am very busy.

Give my love to Nantz.

Believe me W. W. Hope.

J Naylor Esq. **Paris 24th December 1841**
Great Newport Street.
London.

Dear Sir,

Herewith I send you the answers to your different queries. Mr Crosby's legacy is to be fully clear of the legacy duty. The annuity to the viscountess is to be under the restrictions pointed out by you. Only that you will add a legacy to her of twelve thousand pounds to be paid at my demise free of duty (besides the annuity). You will have no occasion for inserting other clauses as Lord Athlone is of age and an English subject. This I will only want as a temporary one, as I shall bring you over a draft of the will for foreign properties, which you will then embody in the general will.

Believe me W. W. Hope.

Chapter Two

January1842 to June 1842

Gate house at Rushton Hall

Mr Moffat. ***Paris 5th January 1842***

Sir,

I have received your letters dated 3rd, 8th, 21st and 31st. You did quite right in putting £1 in the subscription plate at Countesthorpe church.

Has Mr Humphrey the tenant taken the hay on the farm at your valuation?

You will pay for the fifth part of the history of Northamptonshire when you have received it.

Did you sell the filly at Tattersalls? Has the lameness of the old horse disappeared?

Have you started to fill the Icehouse?

Yes, you did well in consulting Mr Markham with your ideas for the Penterglaze mine.

At your first opportunity pay in to the hands of Messrs Harman & Co of Adams Court, Broad Street London, the sum of one thousand pounds.

With regards to the beer, I will write to you in my next letter.

Signed for W. W. Hope.

Messer's Adams and Hooper ***Paris January 13th 1842***

Gentlemen,

I have received you letter of the 14th of December containing a second sketch of the travelling coach. I think the boots of No.1 should have moveable dickies. Though it does not improve the shape, I think the shortening of the carriage in No. 2 is preferable, and that the Imperials divided into five would be best. If you send me a drawing in this manner, I think it will suffice.

Signed for W. W. H.

Mr Moffat ***Paris 21st January 1842***

Sir,

I request you send to London by rail, two cases of bottled beer. Send it to the station with a man and tell him to use the spring cart, but first of all you had better write Brunning to know what would be the most economical way to send it. You will act accordingly when you have the answer. The bottled beer is to be sent to Brunning who is in London acre; he will take care to forward it to me in Paris

Has Blunson entirely quitted the farm?

7th February 1842.

Having been indisposed, I have not been able to answer your different letters sooner. I will now try to answer them.

Pray have you augmented the cottage rents, and do you make Smith and Panter pay rent for their houses?

Have you settled with Mr Blunson and his affairs? He cannot expect his rent to be lower. With regard to what the gardener wants, you may grant it.

Signed for W. W. H.

John Williams Esq. **Paris 7th February 1842.**
Ashford
Middlesex

My dear Sir,

I can assure you that the receipt of your letter gave me a great pleasure, and I should have answered it sooner, but I am sorry to say that I have my poor fathers complaint, the gout, it has been paying me a visit, but I am now re-established and thank god I now generally enjoy good health. I am now thirty-eight, not married and principally live here in Paris, or reside at my seat in Northamptonshire.

I should be most happy to hear from you again through the medium of your daughter or granddaughter.

You will excuse my ignorance, as I lost my parents when I was so young and since that time, I have never met with anyone that could give me information about my father's family. I have lost my three brothers and my eldest sister. She alone left two children, the present Earl of Athlone and his sister. My youngest sister is going on well and has two children. As I said before, I shall be most happy to hear from you and yours and also your welfare.

With every wish for your health and happiness.

Believe me your sincere kinsman, W. W. Hope.

Mr Moffat ***Paris 21st February 1842***

Sir,

I beg you will by return of post tell me the amount of the entire sum of money left in the Harborough Bank and in your hands.

If I understand by the letter of the 18th rightly, you only have £47.5.11 in the bank and £12 in your hands. The rents amounting to £1709.2.8, of which a thousand was paid by you into Messrs Harman's hands. Am I right in supposing that the remaining is £709.2.8 and there remains £47.5.11 for the current expense? I shall be obliged to you to send me an answer as soon as possible, that I may take immediate measures to replace a sufficient sum of money in to your hands, to enable you to carry on operations.

Signed for W. W. H.

Miss N Dunn **Paris February 25th 1842**
13 Berkeley Square.

My dear Nantz,

Brunning is to send the beer on the first steamboat that will take it and that goes to Calais. Underneath is the address he is to put on the cases. In a separate little case, he will put all his bills that I have not got and the drawings that come from Rushton, and address them in the some way. You will write to me when they start. Brunnning will address then to Monsieur William Hope, Aux Soins de Monsieur Dessin, Calais.

Believe me W. W. Hope.

Messrs Harman & Co. ***Paris 28th February 1842***

Gentlemen,

I request that you will pay into the hands of Mr William Moffat, my steward, the sum of five hundred pounds, whenever he shall apply for it, for that sum only.

M Moffat *Paris 28th February 1842*

Dear Moffat,

I have written today to Messrs Harman of Old Broad Street, London, to order the sum of five hundred pounds, to be paid to you whenever you apply for it, to the order of five hundred pounds sterling.

I shall write to you again in a few days time. The five hundred pounds should help you to carry on operations and pay yourself.

Signed for W. W. H.

W. Moffat ***Paris 5th March 1842***

Sir,

I request you will at present and till you receive further orders, suspend all ornamental improvements at the Hall at Rushton. You will only employ the men necessary for your farming operations and to keep everything in good order and proper repair.

Will you be so good as to send me a list of all the horses at Rushton, their ages and their service ability, and those that are not, you will dispose of?

I want the exact amount of all expenditure at Countesthorpe and what you have in hand remaining you will put a valuation on, and what the farm has produced, the two last to be subtracted from the finish, that I may know exactly what has been laid out at Countesthorpe. Also, will you send me the items of your expenses of your first journey to Cornwall? It is a thing I forgot to ask of you when last at Rushton and which I wish to have.

You will not forget in the future to let me know three weeks beforehand when your money runs out? Whenever cottages fall in, could you not augment the rents? Tell Panter he must pay his rents or you will give him notice accordingly. Mrs Hefford does not pay enough rent for her premises.

Signed for W. W. H.

P.S. I wish to have a copy of the agreements of Countesthorpe with regard to ornamental improvements, stop them, but keep planting trees and bushes for improvements.

Miss N Dunn **Paris 5th March 1842**

My dear Nanny,

You are to pay Brunning the sum of £18.19.11 on his giving you a receipt in full of all demands up to the day of you paying him.

I wish you many happy returns of the day on your Birthday.

Believe Me W. W. Hope.

M P Dulinahay **Paris 20th March 1842**
Malinis.

My dear Sir,

I am no sender, and have a great objection to writing and receiving letters, except when necessary. I beg therefore you will consider this letter of mine as final with regard to what it contains.

Your pictures are unfortunately, and you must excuse me if I speak the truth, of a very inferior description and far, very far from being worth even the lowest value you put on them, they are of no use to me.

Your plans for your daughter in law, I am afraid you will find to turn out a failure. I know enough of artists to be able to tell you that only a very few out of many hundred ever succeed.

With regard to you buying pictures for me, I must positively decline any such thing. It is an amusement I keep for myself.

I can only add that if ever an opportunity presents itself to me of getting you eligible employment, you may depend upon me.

In the mean time, believe me, W. W. Hope.

W. N. Moffat. ***Paris 21st March 1842***

Sir,

I have received your letters dated 11th and 13th.It seems to me that it would be desirable for you to keep all the horses except Merrill & Captain and therefore, if they could not be sold, they ought to be shot. All other horses I think you can find work for and keep. I beg you will favour me with your opinion on this matter. Pozey on the pension cannot be counted.

With regards to the lands at Countesthorpe including soil limes and compost, the value of £200 is about right, but you may have overstated the value of it. With regards to letting the farm, you must let it in the most advantageous manner.

I have looked at the plans for the farm, and I have only one objection to the offer. There seems to be a great deal of roof that needs repairing or rebuilding, but you must act as you think proper and to your best judgement.

The beer must be brewed, as the brew is wanted at Rushton. You will have a nine-gallon casks and an eighteen-gallon cask brewed of ale. The beer in the bottles is reserved, but you must tell the brewer that I think the beer is too thick. What can be done to cure it? When the next batch is ready let me know and put some into cases to send to me in Paris. There was two questions in your letter relating to beer but cannot remember what they were.

Signed for W. W. H.

W. Moffat. ***Paris 9th May 1842***

Sir,

Immediately on reception of this letter, you will pay unto Mrs Clarke all wages that are due to her and you will pay her quarterly salary as a mark of satisfaction. I would not part with her for any other reason, but that Brunning has entered my service as house steward and therefore her services are of no further use to me. You will give her every facility in removing her to where she likes and you will give her every assistance in transportation on, of herself, goods and baggage, all as soon as it's convenient to do so.

Write to Brunning, asking him to contact me as soon as he can.

I will write again tomorrow.

Signed for W. W. H.

Mr W Moffat ***Paris 10th May 1842***

Sir,

I have received the enclosed, pray give me your opinion on or tell me what is expected of the land I have in the parish of St Issey?

You will give up to Brunning everything appertaining to the Beer, also the wine cellar.

You may have to alter the flue in the gardener's house, but you will do well to consult Brunning, as he is convergent with flues and chimneys. You have done well letting the park grazing to Blunson as part of his farm.

The coachman is to have one suit of livery and an everyday suit. This should last three years, but one new hat every year. Make a note of this for the future and let this be done regularly.

When Brunning will reside at Rushton and wishes to go to London, he must have full use of the Gig or spring cart, as he may want for transportation of himself or goods. You will arrange the transport at any time he may need it, but it must be at a time most agreeable to you both. Brunning is to have the following for the use of himself and family: Eggs, butter, milk, potatoes, vegetables, poultry, rabbits and the occasional pike from the brook.

I wish to have a good aback of game at Rushton; the keeper had therefore better rear some. You can also keep more rabbits, but let the farmers know or they will complain and want damages. Try to arrange with the farmers to grow some buckwheat in different parts that would be beneficial to the game. Tell them if there is some spare buckwheat seed, you will buy it from them for a profit.

Signed for W. W. H.

H. Benthick Esq. **Paris 18th May 1842**
59 Upper Grovenor
London

I have received on Monday last, your letter of the 11th, announcing the approaching marriage of my niece Lady Elizabeth De Rude Grinkle. I must own that in one point of view, it has been a great disappointment to me.

I had thought, and so had my sister who is at present here with me, what with Elizabeth's fortune and rank, she might have been advised to have married at least an elder son. As everything is now settled, I have nothing more to say on the matter, as it would be perfectly useless.

I have not had the honour of being acquainted with Captain Villers, but I do not doubt that he possesses every quality, which can make me hope that he will ensure Elizabeth's happiness. His birth and family are exceptional and therefore I think I can, with safety, congratulate Elizabeth on her approaching marriage.

You will not be surprised if I decline being named one of the trustees in the marriage settlement, but I have never been consulted at any time, or in any way about Athlone or his sister. It is natural that I should wish that my name should not be made use of, so I therefore enclose my answer to Elizabeth's letter, which I beg you will deliver to her.

Pray give my respects to Mrs Benthick and believe me, W. W. Hope.

Lady Elizabeth De Rude Grinkle **Paris 18th May 1842**
No. 39 Upper Grovesnor Street
London.

My dear Elizabeth,

I am very happy that the first letter you ever wrote to me should be the one announcing the most important and I hope hereafter you will hereafter say the happiest event of your life. It would be a great source of pleasure for me to be present at your marriage.

In all events, I shall be coming to England next month I will come and see you, as I am most anxious to do so and to be acquainted with Captain Villiers, for I have always and always will take a great interest in your welfare, and happiness.

When you write to Athlone, remember me to him, and tell him that when the winter comes and the season's time weighs heavily in his hands, he should come and stay with me Paris.

I do however extend this invitation to both you and your new husband to be. I shall however send an invitation to you both in the future. I hope you will be happy and can both arrange to visit me.

Believe me W. W. Hope.

V. Crosby. **Paris 30th May 1842**

My Dear Crosby,

Herewith a letter from Moffat, which I beg you will return to me and my answer to Moffat, what after having read, I beg you will really forward it to him. This will be a pretty mess. I am afraid that Moffat will not do.

I certainly think Brunnings letter is an impertinent one. You had better say little to him, but instil into his mind that it will not do to offend Moffat because they pull different ways. My interests must suffer, what do you think? This business will bring me shortly to England, I am afraid you have not a very good passage.

Believe me W. W. Hope.

W. Moffat **Paris 30th May 1842**

Sir,

I have received your letter of the 27th of May this morning and though I have little time to spare, I hasten to answer it.

The £150 Mr Brunning's brought you was done by my orders and you will receive it. It is to enable you to carry on operations at Rushton.

I am greatly annoyed to see that you have so misconstrued Mr Brunnings letter of the 9th of March. He certainly has not been bred a scholar, but there is nothing in that letter to question your integrity. I do not approve of your conduct in this matter. You are not acting fairly towards myself. I have put you in a position of a place where you represent me.

If you take offence so speedily and decline on such frivolous grounds of having any correspondence with the heads of my different establishments when necessary, no simultaneous government can be carried on, and my presence would be necessary to pacify any offence that has been given. I repeat you are not acting fairly to me.

I must say that being a good Christian, you must and ought to hesitate before making such judgments on ones fellow creatures. You have been wrong also in letting this anomaly ramble on long in your heart. You should have written to me before now.

The following are my instructions, which you are to execute:

You will go Brunning and tell him how much you felt hurt at his letter. You will explain to him that it appeared to you that he doubted your integrity. Do this with feeling, that of a true Christian and I am positive Brunning will give you the satisfaction of explaining what you desire. You will then see you have been wrong in the instructions you put in his letter. He is industrious, honest and a well-meaning man. You ought to judge him as such. Act honestly towards myself and the best of your judgment.

You and Brunning must understand each other and pull together; I have too many establishments to look after, so I expect you to sort this matter out among yourselves.

Believe me W. W. Hope.

Mr Moffat **Paris 1st June 1842**

Sir,

Following are answers to your letters dated the 22nd and 23rd. You will present my compliments to Mr Wetherall and thank him for his communications.

Will you at once make a survey of all properties touching the Rushton estate and the value of them? I will then know what further steps to take in this matter, e.g. railroads etc.

Has Panter paid his rent? We do not want him to misbehave as he did last year. With regard to the cottages, they can build their own sheds, but you must tell them the design and supply the materials. I shall shortly arrive at Rushton and shall talk this matter over with you then.

You will ask the poultry man to breed extra poultry for fattening. Is Bamford still paid by Brunning? You should only put on extra labour when they are wanted at the hall.

Believe me W. W. Hope.

V. Crosby. **Paris 4th June 1842**

My dear Crosby,

I cannot find any budget for your carriage, should you ask Adams for one? Ask Adams at the same time if my travelling coach is ready? I think I shall be over in London on Friday or Saturday night and then I shall go on to Rushton.

This time I shall want you and Fiffey to go as well and perhaps Nantz. I will certainly want Fiffey to manage Brunning while I am managing Moffat. I shall bring over with me the two Peters and two cooks and Louis.

Forward the enclosed to Brunning after having read it, then seal it. Fiffey had better not have anything from Rushton this time. Brunning not being in the way of it just now, Brunning had better come to London tomorrow.

Give my love to the ladies.

Believe me W. W. Hope.

Mr Brunning **Paris 4th June 1842**

Brunning,

In about ten or twelve days I shall arrive at Rushton. You will get ready the usual rooms and three of the best bedrooms besides my own. I shall have servants with two Peters; two cooks my courier, and me. You will have to engage, for the time I am there, at least two women for cleaning the kitchen and kitchen utensils.

Bamford will put on his livery and come in to the house with you to assist you and it will also be necessary to set on Charles Hefford; if he still employed by you at Rushton, he can carry coals etc. When you employ Hefford and Bamford in the hall, I have written to Mr Moffat to say that you will pay them during the time you employ them for me and the housework. They are not paid from the estate account. Also, order meat on my account ready for the cooks.

Believe me, W. W. Hope.

V. Crosby. **Paris 4th June 1842**

My dear Crosby,

I shall start from Paris on Wednesday evening and shall be in Calais Thursday. As the boat starts at eleven at night I have a monstrous mind to boat it to London, but that depends on circumstances.

When you have read the enclosed put them in the post.

Hannah must explain to Brunning that he must attend to and recollect what is in order now, as I shall not tell him that in future any more, the only notice he will have is that I am coming down small or large establishment.

Has Fiffey got all she needs in vegetables for the house?

My love to the ladies.

Believe W. W. Hope.

Mr Brunning **Paris 6th June 1842**

Brunning,

I am shortly coming over to Rushton, you will not do anything to my bath, but with regards to the blankets, the sooner it is done, the better.

You are to have in the house, but not before Saturday next: Half an ox, one sheep and half a calf. You will apply for the first two from Mr Moffat, who will send them to you, unless he has not got them and so then you will order them from the butcher. That you receive from Moffat in the way of beef or mutton, you will pay him for at then end of the month.

With regards to any articles you receive, you must keep a book in which everything must be recorded. You must order half a sack of very fine flour. Also, get a billiard table ready and see that the lamps are in good order. Direct your letters to London.

Believe me, W. W. Hope.

W. Moffat **Paris 6th June 1842**

Sir,

I have written to Brunning to tell him he is to have in the house on Saturday next (not before), half an ox, one sheep and half a calf. The first two he is to ask you for and as I suppose you have not the last, he is to order it from the butcher. The other half of the ox you will of course dispose of.

I have also told Brunning to pay into your hands at the end of every month the value of the meat delivered by you for the use of the hall. With regard to other articles, he is to keep a book of all that he receives in the way of vegetables, poultry etc.

You will also send for Saturday, ready plucked, twenty-four young pigeons, six old hens, six fat fowl and two fat ducks.

Believe me, W. W. Hope.

Chapter Three

July to December 1842

Keepers Cottage

V. Crosby. **Paris 7th July 1842**

My dear Crosby,

Louis will be in London on Sunday midday, so as to leave London by the first boat that leaves for Calais, which I believe will be Tuesday.

Will you tell Hooper that he must deliver the carriage to Louis at my London house and Hannah is to put three mats in the carriage, and send also the damaged pictures.

Louis will bring a shawl for Nantz. My respects to her Ladyship.

Ever yours truly, W. W. Hope.

V. Crosby. **Paris 8th June 1842**

My Dear Crosby,

Never in all my born days have I been so annoyed. You may tell Hooper that he may keep the new travelling carriage for himself. I really expected it would be entirely finished by now. It was ordered on the 11th of February, four months ago.

I cannot understand how the little carriage can be ready by next Saturday. If he has painted the wheels and axletrees properly, they cannot be dry, and certainly not if you judge by the length of time he takes for the other carriages.

Hooper tells you quite coolly that he hopes to show me the carriage before I leave England. Does he suppose that I built a carriage for amusement. Does he not think that I want it for travelling, and that when a carriage is ordered in the winter, it must be for the summer?

My plan was this: to come over in my own travelling carriage and leave it with Hooper for sundry repairs till September when I return. My intention was to have left England with the new one, as I want it for the 22nd of this month.

Pray ask Hoper what I am to do? My own carriage cannot return to Paris without a thorough repair, which repairs I did not like to have done in Paris. Dam his laziness. I could break every bone in his skin.

The cooks will start by steamboat, which leaves Boulogne tomorrow night at eleven o'clock. I shall certainly want Hannah at Rushton to teach Mrs Brunning about the linen. My respects to her ladyship.

Ever, W. W. Hope.

P.S. Give it to Hooper, he can offer no excuse. Four months ago I ordered the carriage. It's not good enough. Does he suppose that I want the carriage next winter?

W. Moffat **Paris 25th July 1842**

I have received your letters of the 26th of June and those of the 3rd, 10th and 18th of July. In future, you will do well not to deal with Mr Bell again, and you will do well also to fix your prices before hand as people think it always right to compose as much as they can whenever they come into contact with my name.
The ploughman whom you discharged, is it Frith? You will, if so, make him pay rent for his house.
I have looked over the plan of the Desborough estate. I do not think that is eligible. Should any part of it not be sold, let me know.
Has Cockin paid up all arrears? You will be obliged to take care that such a thing does not happen again of keeping back my monies for his own use. You say that the domestic servants have been paid their quarterly salaries. I suppose you mean those at the Hall excepted? I approve of your plans for the farmhouse at Countesthorpe.

In your next letter, tell me if you have taken on an accountant to put the books in order and whether according to my desire you have paid Brunning £500. Pray answer all in your next letter.

Signed for W. W. Hope.
P.S. Have you received the Cornish rents yet?

Mr Moffat. ***3rd August 1842***

I have received your letter of the 26th July. If you think that what Mr Ashby wants for his house ought not be granted, then of course you will not do it.

If I think otherwise, I will let you know, but you must use the best of your judgment.

I forgot to tell you that some of the rails and gates in the park needed painting.

Signed for W. W. H.

Mr Brunning ***Paris 3rd August 1842***

Mr Hope requests Mr Brunning will deliver to Mr Moffat, all papers and letters that arrive at Rushton addressed to Mr Hope. He also wants to know if Mr Brunning has decided anything about the brewing house, as Mr Hope has had no letters from Mr Brunning. Mr Hope wishes to know if Mr Brunning has counted all the windows at Rushton hall and whether by diminishing their numbers, taxes would be saved?

Signed for W. W. H.

(An extract from the letter)

Miss Dunn ***Boulogne 3rd August 1842***

Till the 20th of this month, send all my letters directed to 'Poste Restante, Boulogne Sur Mer. Crosby is staying in Dover.

Signed for W. W. H.

Mr W. Moffat ***8th August 1842***

Sir,

I have received your letter of the 31st July and was considerably annoyed about a part of it. You say "Mr Wetherall kindly obliges to be out on the estate among the Rushtoners in my absence". The next time I am Rushton, I expect Mr Wetherall to be there when I wish to meet him.

Signed for W. W. Hope.

Nicholas Whitley Esq. ***Boulogne 16th August 1842***
Truro
Cornwall.

Sir,

I have received your letter of the 8th and regret I cannot comply with its contents. As long as Mr Moffat acts justly, and for the benefits of my interests, I see no reason why I should take away from him the management of my Cornish properties.

When I last looked at your accounts, I showed Mr Moffat myself several items of expenses of which I did not approve. He has not yet laid before me his observations, but you must make me out a very strong case against him to make me transfer to another person the management of my property.

Signed for W. W. H.

Mr Moffat. ***Boulogne 17th Aug 1842***

Sir,

As the hack stables behind the other stables is very little or ever used or wanted, I request you will put Mr Brunning into immediate proposition of it. Mr Brunning is to arrange for it to be made into a new brew house. Have you recommended building the stables at the back of the house?

I hope you have had the boat put carefully by? If you have any leisure now, you might get back to finishing St Peters spring as soon as labour is free from harvest.

Signed for W. W. H.

P.S. Does the old carriage horse still go lame? Pass this letter to Brunning.

Mr Brunning,

Mr Hope thinks Mr Brunning will do very well to take the hack stable for a new brew house. Brunning must write to Moffat with a full plan for the stable to be made into a brew house.

Mrs Crosby **Boulogne 17th August 1842**

My Fiffey,

As this letter is to speak to Brunning, I must address it to you, as you are a better person to manage Brunning. Besides the disagreeables that Moffat weekly gets me into, here is another fresh one started from Moffat's journey into Cornwall.

Mr Whitley is the agent in Cornwall, under the control of Mr Puckford, and now of Moffat. I have sent his letter for you and Mr Crosby to read with my answer. What he says about the property or the rent increasing is not from his management. It comes from the life leases having expired, which is too long to explain now. Seal my letter to Whitely and forward it and return me Mr Whitley's letter.

I am afraid Moffat's plan is to Quarrel with all the old set and put a new set in, that he might manage in his own way. Would this be as much for his benefit as mine, that is the question.

What has put me on my guard with Moffat is his dislike of Brunning. I can see that very plainly now, that two distinct stewards will always be jealous of each other and never will they pull together. Either Brunning is or is not an honest man. I think him honest, therefore the land steward must be under him, he may well then be able to look after things, and though he may know little or nothing of agriculture matters, his control will be better than none at all. Besides, I can assure you that there will be an immense saving with regard to the housekeeping by this means. I have therefore made up my mind that he ought to be under Brunnings control. I would like to know what you and Mr Crosby's objections to the plan may be.

I wish more to get rid of this troublesome business and all this writing is detestable. It would be most desirable for me to entrust everything to Brunning with proper people under him. Besides another reason, it would give him a work that would always continue; the repairing of the farmhouses etc. This would occupy much of his time at the hall, doing improvements there.

My intention is to come over in October when I shall dismiss Moffat and replace him with a man of Brunnings choice. It would be most desirable and it would be killing two birds with one stone. If not, I should have to come to England again, so therefore, I want you to approve my plan before I meet with Brunning. Brunning is to meet me at your house in Dover where I could tell him of my plan. I could ask him to procure a steward, or bailiff is the proper name. It is important that I should get a person that can do all improvements at the hall and keep full control of affairs.

I have just returned from Brussels and a perilous journey I had too. The heat in Paris and elsewhere is tremendous, no matter where you go everywhere and everything is dried up. I shall leave here on the 23rd, so do not send letters on to Paris after the 21st. All letters to me, will you forward to Dover? Any letters for Brunning, Moffat, Whiteley or Naylor, will you forward them after you have read and wafered them?

We have no need to complain about the weather; it was a beautiful spring and a hot summer, but I hope it will not be too wet this autumn.

Mr Inkson, the tailor was amusing himself the other day. There was not a bed to be had in all this town for love or money. The boats every day from London bring almost 200 people. My complements to Mr Crosby.

Believe Me, W. W. Hope.
P.S. Brunning by this time has received £500. There is no hurry to reply.

Mr Crosby **Boulogne Sur Mer 18th August 1842**

My dear Crosby,

As I thought, Moffats new broom sweeps clean. I think this business he is in is right. If Fiffey sends for Brunning, she had not better begin by pumping him. She knows what she knows of Moffat, and after that consult what ought to be done before we go further.

Return me all answered letters once you had read and wafered them.

Believe me W. W. Hope.

V. Crosby. **Boulogne 21st August 1842**
Care of Captain Ingleson
No. 7 Castle Street
Dover.

My dear Crosby,

I see Hannah has received my letter of the 17th. Tell Hannah to act with Brunning with her very best judgment.

Believe me, W. W. Hope.

P.S. send next letters to Paris.

Mrs Crosby **Paris 8th September 1842.**

My Dear Fiffey,

Tell Brunning that I have received his letter that he must try to have the most eligible person ready to replace Moffat for the 1st October. He must try to get the best place he can, and also as cheap as possible. You can manage all that with him better than myself.

You know I do not like children etc. I should wish a man to come also to have an understanding of how to keep up stables, though I shall always have very few horses, he must understand them and the keeping of the coachman and others in order. It is also desirable that he should write a good hand. That is not so important if he really knows his job, as a bailiff Brunning can take the man occasionally to write up the accounts. I knew the beer at Rushton was bad, therefore, Brunning must manage to have some more made as I shall be there in October. I will dismiss Moffat myself. Till then, the whole thing must be kept a profound secret.

I am just coming back to Paris and I am thinking of starting at the end of the month for London. You may depend on me to be there at the latest by October 1st.

In his letter, Brunning states he has two eligible persons. As he is to be answerable to me, he must please himself in the choice.

My love to Nantz. Ask Mr Crosby if he knows if the guns have been returned to Rushton?

Believe me, W. W. Hope.

P.S. Mr Crosby says you have the 10th or 17th according to the weather, I direct this to London as the glass is going down for storm and it's blowing a gale here.

I forgot to say, will you ask Mr Crosby to inquire at the customhouse if a plated service can be admitted? I know silver plate cannot, but perhaps plated silver dishes might be admitted. As it is not a best set it would be desirable to have the silver service I do not use here taken to Rushton.

Mr Moffat ***Paris 15th September 1842***

Sir,

Herewith you will find a series of questions that I wish to discuss on the same paper. As you have good deal to do, you will do nothing at St Peters spring this year. I perfectly agree with Mr Wetherall that the postman ought to live at Kettering. You will act accordingly. I approve of the new plans for a road to Millers house and at the Wilderness. I intend to be at Rushton for the 1st October. As I shall then want people for the shooting and wish to have no strange workmen about, you will bring all works to a close for that period. Call in all bills and have all the account books ready. This you are particularly to attend. The poultry man is to have plenty of poultry and eggs ready for that time.

Countesthorpe work must close and all bills called in, also for that period, will you give the gamekeeper men to catch the game? Have you settled all the arrears in Cornwall? What determination have you taken with Whiteley? Have you heard anything about the mines lately, and what about the new company that was to be formed?

In your letter of the 14th August, you have put in red ink 'Cash paid to Moffat on account of arrears due lady day 1841'. This I do not understand, Pray explain this. Does the old tenant continue at Countesthorpe or have you got a new one? Have you selected a new tenant for Blunsons farm, and have you given the necessary notice to quit if he has not paid rents due and the arrears? Does the gardener want any seed of any sort? Have you got a list of all the mines in Cornwall?

Signed for W. W. H.

Mrs Crosby ***Paris 29th September 1842***

Herewith is a list of things the cooks will want for Rushton. I shall start on Saturday evening of the weather changes cross over on Monday. Brunning need not come till I write to him. Cooks and two Peters will come over on the London boat with your little carriage. They will have with them an old silver plated service with a valuation of 585 Francs. It's not worth any more and it is for Rushton. Mr Beaugevis and Louis will come with me. I hope Fiffey will like Mr Beaugevis, as she has not met him before. He will have to have a downstairs room. I am glad Mr Brunning has found a Bailiff. I wrote to Brunning to tell him that that I have ordered Moffat to pay into Brunnings hand the £500 he owes him.

Signed for W. W. H.

Mr Moffat **13 Berkeley Square, London, 4th October**
1842
Rushton Hall

Sir,

As you have not have not sufficient funds to pay £500 to Brunning, you need not pay him any as Mr Abbott will be making up the accounts on the 31st.

You will then pay him what is to him and suspend all works immediately and keep as few workmen as you can. You will need to take out a game licence.

I shall be down to Ruston shortly. Get Mr Lambs account up to date and pay what is due to him. I think the game licence has diminished in price due to a change in the law.

Signed W. W. H.

Sir Frances Hollyoake **Rushton Hall, 13th October 42**
Goodrich
Studley Castle
Near Auchester
Warwickshire.

Sir I learn that one of my woods was drawn by hounds this morning without an invitation being sent either by me or my keeper I request that in future if you intend to hunt in the area or my woods due notice must be given to me or my keeper.
You will therefore have the kindness to do so in the future so my keeper will be prepared.

Signed for W.W.H.

John Williams Esq. **Rushton Hall Kettering 27th Oct.**
Ashford
Middlesex

My Dear Sir. I have not written to you though I have received a letter from your daughter which followed me for nearly two months through different posts of Europe as I have been travelling thousands of miles since I last wrote to you, I am now at my place in Northamptonshire where I make only a very short stay as business calls me on the continent again shortly.
While I am here with a few friends we have been shooting and I have sent you today a small basket of game which I hope you will find good, as we rather pride our selves on our game with my kindness regards to Ellen

Believe me W.W.Hope.

Mrs William Stewart **13 Berkley Square 2nd Nov 42**
Aldentiam Abbey
Watford
Hertfordshire

My Dear Cousin,
I have read your letter to my sister attentively, and it has my full appocobation accept in one part, in your explanation why the bequest has been in valid, you have given a reason which in my view of the case is not in accordance with what Mr Harmen my banker and his solicitor Mr Freshfield gave me. I have drawn my pen through that particular part that you may read it over again. In my opinion the bequest is not invalidedated because it has been made payable at 25 instead of 21 years. But because my Aunt out lived my uncle more than 21 years. The law does not allow a bequest beyond that period. Had my aunt Lady Pole only outlived my great uncle Hope, 20 years. There would have been no difficulty I believe about your legacy. The question stands thus If I comprehend it rightly. Your solicitor will tell you if I am right. I have written thus lengthily on the subject as soon as my sister apply to me for an explanation. It would be very necessary that yours and mine should accord.

I shall be happy to see you and Anna and your family whenever an opportunity may occur, but I do not think there is a likely hood of it. My stay in London is always short as I am never there but on business or on my way to Northamptonshire & it is generally at a time of the year when you are out of town.
But I have not the kind affection of your mother to myself I shall always retain grateful recollection of it & a great for yourself and sister as being associated with my early recollections.
With my kindness regards to Anna

Believe me W.W. Hope
P/S I leave for Paris tomorrow my address is 121 Rue Dominique.

Mr Moffat ***London 5th October***

Sir, I shall arrive at Rushton Friday next. I request that you have in your hands all the money you can collect, including what is in the bank and elsewhere.

Brunning will want to order a good stock of poultry and the keeper is to shoot a few brace of partridges for Friday. A dozen pigeons are to be sent in on Saturday morning. The keeper is to send two leverets and some rabbits in the house for Friday and the poultry man must find 500 eggs.

Signed for W. W. H.

Mr Whiteley ***Rushton Hall 30th October 1842***
Truro

Sir,

I have to inform you that Mr Moffat has quitted from my service, and has now been replaced by Mr J Brunning to whom all communications will be addressed.

Signed for W. W. H.

A Lake in the Rushton Hall grounds

St Peters Spring, in the Hall grounds

Chapter 4

January to June 1843

The Ice House, Rushton Hall

Mr Brunning **Paris 1843**
Rushton

I forgot to mention to you in my last letter that Mr Hope wished to have your account book, neatly, well written by the clerk, that you are to employ for that purpose, and you are to send me a copy over every three months, in a summary:
What the accounts of receipts and expenditure is at the hall.
What the keepers expenses are.
The poultry, gardens and farming are all to have there own balance sheet, as all things that belong to Mr Hope must be on their own accounts for the estate.

Mr Hope would like to know just what has been done at Rushton since he was last there and that you must write to inform him every ten days. Mr Hope wishes to know what is going on in the village and county in the way of information and gossip and news. By this means, Mr Hope will be able to communicate on any subject that might strike him. You must be in full knowledge of all the letters he sends you.

P.S. Mind when you go to Cornwall, should any papers be sent to the London house or when you are not at Rushton, tell Mrs Brunning to forward them to the London house to Miss Dunn. She will then keep them for you or forward them to me. Keep a book at the house to keep all correspondence in it of what you have at Rushton.

Signed for W. W. H.

Mr Brunning **Paris 31st January 1843**

Mr Hope has requested me to mention to you again just how much he was dissatisfied with his keeper's dogs; they are really not worth keeping. It is absolutely necessary that the keeper should find better dogs for the next shooting season and you must tell him so.

Mr Hope is likewise determined to allow no more dogs than the following numbers to be kept at Rushton, with the exception of two housedogs; one pointer, two retrievers, three spaniels and they must all be of exceptional quality and in perfect working condition. Mr Hope will have no more breeding or puppies kept; nothing but dogs that know well their work and are able to perform well. You must be very firm about this with your keeper, Mr Hope is determined to have a few dogs but they must be excellent quality.

With respect to your letter to Mr Cockayne-Maunsell, in which you charge him with trespassing onto Mr Hopes estates and of which the sole shooting over has been succeeded to Mr Hope by the owners. Almost the same thing, Mr Maunsell had no business where he was. Should you however write to him again or to any one else about any unpleasant occurrences taking place at Rushton, it would be much better for you (to give Mr Hopes opinion) to employ Mr Lamb, a solicitor of Kettering, to write to him a caution, a polite letter, of which you are to copy in your own hand before he sends it to Maunsell or any other. When a lawyer writes a letter, there is never any danger of its being laid hold to, or twisted to mean anything else, other than that the lawyer chooses. These lawyers in Northamptonshire are very sharp fellows, if they can endeavour to get windward of you by their minds, they will get around things in one way or another.

Therefore, you had better employ Mr Lamb to write to answer on this most dislikeable subject, or you can ask him to write a letter for you and you copy it out in your handwriting, that might be best.

Signed for W. W. H.

Mr Brunning ***Paris 13th February 1843***

I beg to inform you that the pheasants arrived in good order. Since I departed from London nine weeks ago, we have not seen any letters from you. Mr Hope says in future you will write in the 15th of each month, a full summary of works expenses and income at the hall.

Whenever you go to London, you must take with you as many things as you can without being charged extra baggage such as eggs, poultry, butter, vegetables and pigeons or whatever Rushton may produce. Mr Hope wishes to know how many poultry you have and how much butter you make and the price you get for it.

Signed for W. W. H.

Mr Brunning ***Paris 16th February 1843***

Mr Hope received your letter if the 10th. On reflection, Mr Hope thinks it better if you do go to the London house before the 15th April. That will give you time to finish the brewing without interruptions. When brewing has finished, you will send some to me in Paris in a nine-gallon cask. Forward it and some more oranges to Mr Dessin of Calais.

Send Mr Hopes apology for not informing Mrs Bosworth that my keeper went on her estate without informing her first. We have changed stewards tell her, so that was where the confusion laid. As we wish to Keep on good terms with her for the sake of the shooting and should the farm come for sale, see if you can find her a turkey or some extra good game, for your sake, visit her with a good gift so that this incident will all be soon forgotten.

A keeper in the service of Mr Hope can keep a cow or horse and have as many rabbits as he wishes. This will be stopped if he is no longer employed by Mr Hope and he will start to pay rent.

In the past, Mr Hope has given to the poor of the village, but Mr hope thinks that this must not be seen as an annual event, but Brunning, you are to use your judgement to give to the poor coal or wine if they are ill. The coal must not be a regular gift.

I will give you advice on how to send the beer as soon as it is.ready, and the best way to send it.

Have you filled the icehouse?

Should you have any disagreements in the future, you can say you are acting on Mr Hopes orders.

Signed for W. W. H.

Mr Brunning ***February 28th 1843***

When any notice of grand jury in Northamptonshire take place that interests me you must write to me, any other legal or jury problems, you must consult Mr Lamb.

The keeper's dogs are good for nothing. He must use his legs to get better in Northamptonshire; he must walk over neighbouring counties till he finds some. Other people have good dogs, why not Mr Hope?

You are to brew sufficient beer of quality to supply Rushton Hall and the London house during Mr Hope's residence there. The table beer for London is to be in eighteen-gallon casks and the other in to nine-gallon casks. You are to have made at Rushton, six stands for placing the beer in the London house and also do not forget the steps, which were ordered to be made for the cooks larder in the London house. Take care not to put your beer into new casks. You are to purchase as many new beer barrels as will be necessary.

Let me know what you have done respecting the coachman? Also, whether you have sold the farm horses and will you want the use of the pony as you requested? It will be the same deal as last time. Should you have changed the coachman, you must get a hard working, sober man that can drive well. Are you still looking for someone to put in the lodges?

Once you have filled the icehouse, you or others must not enter, it is to be hermetically sealed as possible. Whenever you need to go to London, you are to send over another chest of oranges, but you must select them and try one first as the last ones were sour, although they looked fine.

Signed for W. W. H.

Mr Brunning ***Paris 9th March 1843***

Sir,

In respect of your letter of the 27th February, I duly note the contents every year, for the last seven years at least, the keepers' constantly asked permission of Mr Hope to keep the same dogs, bad as they were, for the next ensuing shooting season. They were quite a disgrace. No dogs could have been uglier nor more unwork like, yes they were a disgrace. In fact, the keeper must find better. Be will be out of a job himself if he cannot find better. He must walk all over Northamptonshire in search for some, then if he cannot find any, go in to Leicestershire. If then he does not succeed, then he must walk over to Norfolk and if none are found, then he will venture into Scotland and search till he finds them and he must not return with out them. Mr Hope is determined to have the best dogs kept only. You must make an agreement if necessary with the keeper about what he needs. Pay him an extra cost during his time away in searching for the dogs.

Mr Hope will be coming over in the spring and will expect to see the new dogs well tried and working. Mr Hope wants no more ill bred dogs like past ones. All he can say is that they were the ugliest brutes he had ever seen or set eyes upon, they had a curse on them and they were afraid of even a hedge. The Keeper may keep a retriever of the old stock that is to have pups and the keeper can then sell them, as he thinks that they were so good and valuable, he might get over the money for them, and what he will gain, buy some good stock. I read the observations sent at once and note, dogs to be kept at Rushton are one pointer, two retrievers, three spaniels.

How are the cooks going to convey the water at the hall? How are you managing the water for the gardens? Has Mr Wetherall done anything towards exchanging the lands in the park? Are there any more dead people in the village since Mr Hope was there, if so who? Keep a record of any empty cottages due to deaths, but on no account do anything that is the duty of the parish to look after and fulfil. Inspect the new hedges along the roadsides near the new barn. The discovery, which Mrs Brunning made about the mismanagement of the dairy, is one that I was glad to hear of. Now the wife of the bailiff can be superintendent of the dairy and the poultry yards under the direction of Mrs Brunning as Mrs Brunnings time is too valuable to spend time with that occupation.
Mr Hope hopes you will purchase plenty of poultry for the spring so that the stock can supply the London house. You will both breed and buy them. It's better to have too many than too few, you can always sell them. It was a good ideal to improve the osier beds. When will you be sending beer? Do you like your casks well seasoned?

When you come back from Cornwall, Mr Hope requests you send for eating, a chest of oranges and satsumas. The oranges must be of the Saint Michael, as they are really the best. Send some for eating and some for keeping. The last ones you sent had thin skins, no pips and were really sweet.

Mr Hope has got some endive seed for the gardener. Send Mr Hope a list of seeds the gardener will need at Rushton. Mr Hope wishes to sell the two carriage horses at Rushton, try to get £130 for the two. When you have sold them Mr Hope will send over two more.

Has anybody died peacefully in the Maunsell family? Are you short of money yet?

Mr Hope thinks you should not go to London till the had season is finished, then he has time to make changes at the London house.

When you find a new bailiff, find one who has a wife that is willing to work and who you can place every confidence in and can manage in your absence. Mrs Brunning will be the superintendent when you are away.

Any new bailiff must have a wife that is trustworthy and a worker and they must be able to set the hens on eggs and be in full charge of the poultry.

Write to let Mr Hope know if you cannot sell the carriage horses, even if you have to sell them for as little as £30 each.

What has the keeper done with those bad dogs? Has he sold them, shot them or even hung them? We never want to see them again, as they did not pay for their keep. The Keeper must be back at Rushton hall by the breeding season. Have you got the fishing licence?

You said in your last letter you could not buy the pipes you wanted for the spring. It is important that you get the water working, no time must be lost. You had better go and see Mr Weatherall and ask him whether he has taken any steps to the adjustments of the church ponds in the park.

Will Bamford be able to attend the sheep? The mutton that we had last year was not much good.

Signed for W. W. H.

Miss Williams **Paris 10th April 1843**
Northaw
Near Barnet

My dear Kinswoman,

I feel very sincerely obliged to you for the letter you wrote to me on the death of my poor nephew Lord Athlone and for the many kind expressions of feeling, which you evince for this untimely loss. It was indeed a very unexpected event.

I was most happy to hear that your father's health continues to be so good at his advanced stage of his life. I hope sincerely that he may continue the same for a very long time under your affectionate care and attention.

Pray remember him to me.

Believe me, W. W. Hope.

Mr Inkson **Paris 20th April 1843**
Tailor of London

I am requested by Mr Hope to inform you that his steward is going to Paris in a week's time. He begs therefore, that you will have his clothes ready within forty-eight hours of receiving notice of when Brunning will arrive to collect them. Those that you cannot get ready in time, you will take to Mr Hopes house at 13 Berkeley Square. If you cannot finish them, then they can be finished off in Paris at all cost to you, as work is expensive in Paris.

Signed W. W. H.

Mr Brunning **Paris 3rd May 1843**

Mr Hope does not intend to visit England this spring. He has a great many things to explain to you that is impossible to inform you in writing. So he thinks it better you come over to Paris.

On receipt of this letter you will leave Rushton for London, Where upon your arrival, Miss Dunn will give you some new clothing that is for Mr Hope. You will bring it over mixed with your apparel and wearing it in order to get it through the Calais customs house. Mix it well so that they do not know. Also can you bring with you: four best Yorkshire hams, some tongues, and a chest of oranges, provided they are as good as they were last time.

Mr Hope wants you to also bring over your account books so he can see if they are kept as he wishes. If the books are not as Mr Hope wishes, he will be pleased to show you how he wants them done.

Take the direct steamboat from London to Calais, then proceed to the hotel Dessin, where Mrs Dessin on Mr Hopes orders, will pay you £500 for the expenses of the journey. You and your baggage will take the Diligence to Paris. Let me know what boat you hope to come over on.

The keeper is to breed as many pheasants and partridges as he can, tell him he can catch some wild ones and clip their wings.

Only catch the fast London Calais boat and also can you bring from London some three pink and three red Rhododendrons and some beer.

Signed for W. W. H.

Mr Brunning **Paris 4th May 1843**

Enclosed is a letter that you will take to Mr Dessin at Calais and he will then give you £500 out of that money. Mr Dessin will pay any customs duty due and any costs due to him you will also pay to him.

Can you also bring over fifty of the finesse Dahlias and some ten Paveraliuma and if you cannot get the Rhododendrons I mentioned in my last letter, then do not bring any at all.

When you arrive in Calais, ask Mr Dessin to cost the transport to Paris of the goods. I think it will be too costly by the Diligence. You must then send them by the haulage Accelere, but you are on no account to come on any transport other than that of the London - Calais service.

Signed for W. W. H.

Jeremiah Hartman Esq. **Calais 12th June**

My dear Sir,

I can assure you that it is with feeling of gratitude that I received your letter, but I am happy to say that I think no alarm need be felt on the subject.

I have invested a very large sum on landed property in this country. I have at this moment lands for sale in Paris, insured for sale to the value of £60,000, but I think it is worth £70,000. In order to make another property for sale I have been obliged to make some sacrifices and I will have to make some more. All things will eventually fall into place. When I have sold these, I shall reinvest in England. In order to cover all I have owing to you at your house, I therefore wish to dispose of my Russian stock, sufficient to produce £50,000. This should be more that enough to square things up and reinvest. Will you be so kind as to inform your house of my intentions and direct them to sell what you think will be the most eligible? Should it be necessary for me to sign any papers, I beg they will be forwarded to me. It is not my intention to come England at the present, but in July and August, I shall be in Germany.

I repeat my dear sir, that I am infinitely obliged to you for the kindness you have shown me, and believe me to remain always with great regards for you.

W. W. Hope.

V. Crosby **Paris 14th June 1843**

My dear Crosby,

I had your papers here this morning. It is really beautiful weather here, but I see the glass is going down again, and I suppose that we shall have some scorching weather again. It rained very hard on St. Medards day, at the same day here as St. Swithen in England.

The following are observations for Brunning:

The only dog I can do without is a pointer he is the most unnecessary. Has the keeper been to Norfolk to try and find some dogs?

Ask Brunning if it is really necessary for me to give anything for the broken bell, for which Mr Weatherall has given £4. How much must I give?

As soon as Brunning receives the rents, he must pay £400 to Fiffey for the London house. Nothing ought to be written about the foxes, but in a private letter from Brunning.

Miss Maunsell and her dogs have been disturbing the game the keeper tells me. We must get rid of her with the greatest civility. Get Mr Wetherall to have a civil and polite word about it with her.

My love to Hannah. I hope she has got out of her misery. My duty to Miss Nantz and beg she will write to me all the things I have sent, so that can learn the English terms. Would you believe it, there is an English couturier here who is employed by all the elegancies. She makes things so well and is very good at the task.

Believe me W. W. Hope.

V. Crosby **Paris 18th June 1843**

My dear Crosby,

I am heartily glad that both you and Hannah got over so well. We have beautiful weather here. I told the man at the club to send you the Moniteur Parisian, have you received it ? Are there any more newspapers you would like? I shall ask Chevalier at the club what it will cost to send them; just say what you want and I can send it, but the Moniteur Parisian costs 10 Sous. This you will have to pay Hannah for.

The tailor has got me a coat, a pair of Brownies and a waistcoat, which he is to return; the boots he must keep them. Tell Hannah that I pay 10 Sous for washing my shirts here, so therefore in London I should get them washed for the same price.

I have received your letter of the 15th. I'll read it and answer it word by word. I am quite surprised the keeper cannot find any dogs. Everything can be found with money. I am sure I could get them. I do not agree with you about having more than two retrievers. We have always managed to shoot with only one and a bad one at that. Pray tell why I should want more?

Tell Hooper that he is perfectly wrong about the carriage springs. It is that they are perpetually snapping off at the axletrees at the three screw placings. I do not know if is the same with your carriage, but the large travelling carriage seems to be free of that problem. Master Hooper must think I am an old woman to keep treating me so. He should refer to his new ideas. Pray ask Hooper if it was the fault of the people here that the axle on my new Cabriolet broke. Have you shown it to him?

Believe me W. W. Hope.

V. Crosby **Paris 21st June 1843**

My dear Crosby,

I have received you letter from Hooper. Tell him he must make the springs as I wish. He must make them for the travelling coach, as it is to have a water closet, it is to be made to my designs. I do not approve of his making of the water closet and the place next to it in one. They must be separate and also they are to let down from the inside when they are not wanted or travelling. They must be of strong boards that can be easily taken out and the space covered in strong board instead.

I think Inksons bill is too much. I shall return to the French tailors for the most fashionable, and those who make as well as Inkson are five and twenty per cent cheaper.

We have had just two days rain and now back to fine weather again.

Believe me, W. W. Hope.

V. Crosby Paris 24th June 1843

I advise you in the future to take an entire sheet of paper as however carefully it is wafered and opened the paper gets torn and part of the letter gets illegible.

I shall come over two or three weeks before the shooting season and before my shooting party. The latest date the carriage must be ready is the 15th October. I suppose you can take the carriage with you to the place where you are going to stay, then send it back directly to Hooper or take it back yourself with all the empty boxes. Hooper could make all the alterations and then you could have it back again for you and Hannah to come up to town in. Tell Hooper I want a drawing of the new springs, I want to see if he understood me. Also, ask him how much new wheels would cost and how much he would give for the old ones.

With regard to the shooting blouse, I will have one made when I come over. I shall have plenty of time.

Believe me, W. W. Hope.

P. S. I suppose it will not come to much sending the carriage back if there is no railroad. Ives would be glad I suppose to employ two old horses.

I should wish to make a present to somebody of a very fine large setter who will retrieve and point. I still need a good new dog. Can the Keeper or Brunning find one? Tell Hooper the Cabriolet was built by him in 1834. He must keep very bad account books if he cannot find it.

V. Crosby **Paris 29th June 1843**

When I come over to England, I will myself inspect the mattresses and I think I shall be able to manage them when I am there. They require three months sleeping on them to make them comfortable. When you are not using them, be sure to put boards on them, equally all over with some weights on them when new, to press them down level. I am certain I can make a good bed for you. It would be expensive to have the bed, its frame and two old women to come over and make a mattress. Last year Brunning succeeded in making a very good mattress either for London or Rushton, I forget which.

I hope you resolved the matter of the young lady riding on my grass and disturbing the pheasants.

I have received some cloth from Inkson.

Believe me, W. W. Hope.

Old road bridge in the Hall grounds, at one time the road to Glendon and Rothwell

Horse and carriage at Rushton Grange

Chapter five

July 1843 to December 1843

Hope Arms now the Thornhill Arms, built by Hope

Mr Hooper **Paris 1st July 1843**

Sir,

You will make the alterations to my carriage springs in accordance with my instructions and drawings contained in the letter of the 27th. You will also make a cover to fit over the weight which can be put in the carriage when it is doing town work and taken off for travelling, but that means you must make stronger springs.

The carriage is to be repainted as you suggest and with regards to the cushions and lining of the coach box etc, it is to be made entirely of ash leather. If necessary it may be altered to match, and the axles to remain as they are.

I think after all, you had better fit new tyres on the wheels. With regard to the water closet, I shall come and advise you when I come to England. This should not prevent you from finishing the carriage entirely.
Believe me, W. W. Hope.

Mrs Crosby **Paris 6th July 1843**

My dear Hannah,

It certainly seems to me very extraordinary that Brunning does not do a mattress well. You must write to him and tell him that if he cannot do better, then I shall have him over here to make him learn till he can make a good one himself, even if it takes six months. I am determined to have good beds.

A good bed should be of a straw mattress, a hair mattress and two mattresses. It should be like the one Mr Verning has. Mr Crosby could do well by looking at that one. He could then do not harm by telling Brunning just how to make one, as I insist upon every bed being made properly, as I have several gentlemen coming over this year and I would be excessively displeased if he cannot make beds properly.

Tell Mr Crosby to write to Mr Dessin to make arrangements about the carriage. It will be sent to him in his name as he is a French man with a hotel in Calais. It will not be fully painted by Hooper and the boxes will be old ones fitted. It will also go over from Dover. Tell Dessin that if it travels in his name it's possible that the customs will not notice that it is a new carriage and not make the tax duty on it.

We have had two weeks of very dry and cold winds and now it's a very hot south east wind and we are all drying up.

Tell Brunning to start to Cornwall to collect the rents as soon as he has finished the haymaking.

Give my love to Nanny and believe me, W. W. Hope.

P.S. Schard has had another fall from one of those young horses.

V. Crosby **Paris 10th July 1843**

Mr Beaugeois has seen nothing of the man of the Mouiteur de la mode. Send me the address of the office which is his paper, that there may be no mistake and I will send to know what there is to pay. Joseph has seen nobody at all.

Will you ask Brunning if he will send the coachman to London to learn to drive. If he can get a beautiful dog, well broke and who will point and carry or fetch (I do not know the term) I should like Brunning to buy him.

Has the keeper got any dogs? Has Brunning got a bailiff. What does he intend doing with the back gates?

My love to the ladies and tell Hannah I will follow her advice about the mattress. Enclosed is a paper which you will put in with my will and to be opened by you after my death.

Believe me, W. W. Hope.

V. Crosby **Paris 17th July 1843**
27 Spencer Parade.
Ramsgate.

My dear Crosby,

You did right in writing Brunning as you did. When you write, tell him:
First, he ought to say if the weather is good or has been bad. Second, he has never written a word about the game, if the breeding was good or bad and how many the keeper is rearing. Thirdly, something about what he is doing in a farming way. Fourthly, in short, his letters ought to contain more information about what he is doing about the farming business work at the hall and about the game, when he cleans the lakes and what building will need repairs. In short, he ought to give much more information.

We still continue to have beautiful weather here, such weather as Fiffey would like.

Believe me, W. W. Hope.

V. Crosby. **Paris 25th July 1843**

When you left Paris I gave you some papers of which I wanted answers. There was something about the guns, what was it?

Have you tasted Brunnings beer that is in London, how is it? I suppose he sent you some, if not, he must do so.

With regards to the coachman, Brunning may let him remain, but I shall most likely discharge him after my departure from England. I have very strong objections to any relation of Brunnings wife working there, as it can be very disagreeable if you have to discharge them. I have not had a letter from Brunning about his bailiff. Yes, I greatly approve of his idea about locking the front gates when I am absent, with regards to the back gates, he must please himself.

Believe me, W. W. Hope.

V. Crosby **Paris 26th July 1843**

Dear Crosby,

Can you return the bailiff letter to me? I am afraid that Brunnings stubbornness in not choosing to have an under bailiff will subject me to much inconvenience. I am beginning to despair about Brunning. You will know as soon as I got the under bailiffs letter, just what I thought. Brunning seems to me to be nervous about what I think of his in think of his integrity. That's not what he ought to be nervous about. He ought to be nervous about what I shall tell him about getting a bailiff. I am extremely angry with him for not writing and telling me about Mr Lambs opinion about discharging the bailiff. I am positive a paper from me is necessary and out of fear of having done wrong in not engaging him in his name. He does not like to ask for my signature. If that is his game, then it is unpardonable.

Believe me, W. W. Hope.

Mr Williams — ***Minnel 8th August 1843***
Shuttleworth
Bedfordshire

Sir,

In answer to your letter of July 5th 1843. This is to inform you that it was by my orders that Mr Brunning has dismissed you. He is to pay you what he owes you and you are to then vacate my property.

Signed for W. W. H.

Mrs Crosby — **Paris 8th August 1843**

My dear Hannah,

In answer to your letter on the 5th July and herewith I return Brunnings letter. I will take care that he shall not know I have read it. I will send you some observations, which you will make to him or not, just as you and Mr Crosby think proper. I see from Brunnings letter that he has heard of a dog. I should like to know all about it and its price as soon as possible.

Have the crop of turnips come through, and has Brunning finished cutting the vegetation? I have had the good fortune to settle some more bills with great determination and I managed to find the famous history of Greene for Mr Crosby.

Believe me, W. W. Hope.

Messrs Harman and Co. — **Chateau De Duras**

Gentlemen,

I have for the first time today been able to open my letters as I have had brain fever, which I am pleased to say has left me out of danger.

I have no objection to your lending term, as I shall soon have a sale and end the debt.

Believe me, W. W. Hope.

Mr Buller — ***Paris 1st October 1843***
Boulogne.

I received your letter here on my arrival last night. A few days after my departure from Holland I was served with a severe illness on my road here, which confined me to my bed for ten days.

It would be very useless for you to come and meet me in Paris, as at this moment I am perfectly incapable of attending to any business. I will attend to Mrs Stewarts business as soon as possible.

Signed for W. W. Hope.

Messrs Harman and Co. — ***16th December 1843***

I have received your letter dated the 2nd December. I am sorry I have not been able to answer it as I have been confined to my bed with rheumatic gout for the last eight weeks. It is within the last few days that I have been able to use my hands.

Should there be any Russian bonds unsold, you had better sell them and inform Mr Crosby at my London house at 13 Berkeley Square.

Signed for W. W. Hope

Chapter Six

January to December 1844

Rushton Church tower, repaired in 1844. Hope donated £5 towards the repairs

Henry Freshfield Esq. ***Paris 4th January 1844***
New Bank Buildings
London

Sir,

I have at length after having been confined to my bed, ever since I last saw you, recovered the use of my hands sufficiently to write to my sister Mrs De Heeckeren. There remains of the whole matter of her seat in Holland. You or one of your persons must go to Holland to se her to appraise the matter and agree.

Signed for W. W. H.

Messrs J. C. Freshfield Esq. **Paris 6th January 1844**

Gentlemen,

Yesterday I received your letter of the 3rd. I was agreed between myself and Mr Freshfield in the last conversation I had together, that he or any other gentleman of your house would think proper to go over to the Baroness with the deed for her signature. She would then read her marriage contract, shown her by him and her notary. This I have communicated to her and I now cannot change anything, and I believe it would be unless to try, as I know the Baron has a strong objection to sending over their marriage contract.

Believe me, W. W. Hope.

Edward Harman and Co. **Paris 10th February 1844**
London

My dear Sir,

You will easily concern how distrusted I felt when I learnt the melancholy news contained in your letter. The affectionate and grateful regard I felt for your brother was but too natural and in him the loss cannot be replaced. My consolations can be offered to your sister for such a loss. I beg you will tell her how deeply I feel for her on this sad occasion. Pray present my kindest regards to your brother.

Believe me, W. W. Hope.

To the Governor and Company **Paris 18th March 1844**
of the Bank of England.

I William Williams Hope of Trevorrick in Cornwall Esq. do give notice in pursuance of the resolution of the house of commons paper 8th March 1844 that it is my desire to signify my intent to receive £3.5s per cent annuities and new £3 per cent annuities in accordance with the said resolutions, with respect to £3,000 £3.10s annuities 1818 now standing in my name.

W. W. H.

Mrs Stewart **Paris 2nd April 1844**
18 Hill Street, Berkeley Square, London

My dear Cousin,

I have to thank you and Anna for your offer of my mother's miniatures, for which I feel grateful. I am sorry I have no room for them here, but I would be obliged if you could send them to my London house at 13 Berkeley Square.
Pray give my love to Anna. Believe me, W. W. Hope.

Chapter Seven

January to December 1845

The elegant Barouche

Messrs Adams and Hooper **Paris 6th May 1845**

Gentlemen,

You perfectly misunderstood my last letter when I said you might cut the hind part of the body. I meant you should cut it away from the sides as well as behind, therefore from the body. Thus I proposed making it thus, but I think after all it will adopt your drawing number six with the crafted axle, thus this carriage need not be built for one horse, but make it as light and comfortable as possible, and give it all the width you can. I beg you pay particular attention to the stuffing of the back seat.

All your carriages have the some defects. You cannot lean back with your hat on, or the ladies with their bonnets on, so I beg you to pay particular attention to this, so that one can lean backward, the back part of the head can be seen over the padding of the back seat. If you do not understand me let me know.

I wish also to know if you considered a cranked axle or would this upset the design of the springs? It would be best painted dark green or olive, which ever you think looks best and lined in morocco not cloth. The lining could be green.

This carriage I consider you can build for £170, everything included, including the Collins patent axles trees. I must have no outside items; everything to be included in the price and loose no time in building it as I want this carriage directly. Write me the answer by the return of post.

What cannot be lined with morocco could be lined with strong silk, but use morocco as much as you can. Let me know if you have any objections to the front and hind axles being the same width as they have to go on very bad roads. They would be best to finish the same width as the carriage.

Believe me, W. W. Hope.

Messrs Adams and Hooper **Paris 10th May 1845**
London

Gentlemen,

It seems that you quite misunderstood my letter of the 6th. You say that you make the heads to fall much flatter. This has nothing to do with the question, I suppose the head up. I want the back part of the carriage stuffed in the manner that the rim of my hat may go over it, to allow me to sit and lean back.

In my town chariot, I cannot lean back with my hat on without crushing the rim, or without crushing the ladies bonnets. In this country, they manage better by making the back seat padding lower. This allows the lady or gentleman to lean back without being inconvenienced. I do not know if I have made myself sufficiently well understood, so you must calculate the height of the back and then allow some neck to be seen, so the rim of the hat or bonnet is well clear of the seat back. Could you not line the sides of the head with morocco and the rest with some cloth that must be strong enough? The doors morocco and cloth curtains to the heads.

You have not sent me a plan of the springs I wanted and you did not say if you were fitting a crop spring or not under the carriage. You may have to adjust the price to let me know if everything is included. I want common locks on all the boxes with a master key to open all of them.

Believe me, W. W. Hope.

V. Crosby **Paris 16th May 1845**
13 Berkeley Square
London.

The price for Rushton estate is £250,000. I will not take less, though it cost me about £142, 000, it is worth a good deal more now. I have rebuilt the hall and the park wall, improved the lands out of the park, rebuilt the farm houses and bought all the fields that I could get around my woods that would improve the shooting. I have not cut down a single tree, but I have made plantations for game cover.

I wish to sell all the furniture and some pictures that I saved from the fire, also the contents of the cellar. I will keep the best sherry and the silver plate, some of the contents of the library and some family pictures and prints and my old bureau. I do not wish to have a auction sale, but the price must be all included £250,000,

Write to Brunning of the wording, and tell him to come up to London as I want to see him on business.

Believe me, W. W. Hope.

Messers Adams & Hooper **Paris 16th May 1845**

Gentlemen,

I find when the sides of my Barouche (when they are up), if lined with cloth is very disagreeable to my face to lean against and it is not padded, the wood hurts my head.

I would like the sides therefore to be in morocco and slightly padded. I suppose that your price included the budget and drag? Lose no time in the building of the carriage and let me know when it will be finished.

Believe me, W. W. Hope.

Mr Boi **April 10th 1845**

I regret extremely I cannot give a favourable answer for repairing the road at the Mennil. Whenever I have the honour of seeing you, I will explain my reason. I should have had much pleasure in doing so on Sunday next, if I had gone to the Mennil, but I will do so at the first favourable opportunity.

Believe me, W. W. Hope.

Honourable Mrs Maunsell **Mennil Le Boi**
Thorpe Malsor Hall
Kettering.

My dear Madam,

When I last saw my steward, he asked me to grant him the use of the hall for putting a great quantity of furniture and bedding there and he asked my permission not to have the hall shown, as it would not be in a fit state to be seen. This I doubt not, to be the cause of the refusal you met with, which I regret very much. I have written to him to say whenever you wish to see the hall, you can write to him and arrange a meeting time when he would be willing to show you the hall.
I thank you for inquiring about my health, which is still indifferent.

Believe me, W. W. Hope.

Mr V. Crosby **Paris 15th June 1845**

Brunning will leave London by the steam boat for Calais on Thursday 23rd. He will find somebody waiting for him at Calais with a letter from me. It will be Jeandel my groom. All that he cannot take with him in the carriage must be well packed, so as to send it by haulage to Paris.

Brunnings accounts were well drawn out this time. Let me know when he wants some more money.

Believe me, W. W. Hope.

P.S. Let me have all the remaining pheasants killed and brought over with him.

Mr Crosby ***Paris 27th June 1845***

There seems to be some misunderstanding between the occupiers of my farms at Rushton about killing the rabbits. This is to give them notice that Mr Brunning is to strictly enjoy them. They are not to kill the rabbits themselves, but should any damage be done by my rabbits, they will be appraised of it and Brunning will do the necessary. Should any permission ever be granted by Moffat or Mr Puckford, it is contrary to my express orders and if such a thing was permitted, it is high time such a misunderstanding of my wished should cease.

Signed for W. W. H.

Harman & Co. **Clig La Chapelle 16th August 1845**
Bankers

Gentlemen,

The letter to yourselves and Mr Freshfield is in perfect accordance with the order I sent to my steward Mr Brunning at Rushton, and I have to thank you for your prudence in this matter. I have requested therefore, that the title deeds will be shown to you before depositing with the Bank of England. Make sure you keep a copy of additions and alterations.

Believe me, W. W. Hope.

Thomas P H Maunsell Esq. **Paris Nov 5th 1845**
Thorpe Malsor
Kettering.

My dear Sir,

I beg to offer you my very sincere thanks for the very kind offer of your good offices towards myself contained in your last letter of 2nd and of which you may rest assured I shall avail myself at the very first opportunity. I had been in hopes that on my last visit to the country we could have cleared up the matter of the railroads. They are abominable and hateful when they come near your dwelling. I hope and trust that our neighbourhood nevertheless will remain clear and quiet and will not be interrupted by them.

Believe me, W. W. Hope.

Chapter 8

January to December 1846

A steam engine of the period at Kettering Station

Miss Williams **Paris 6th February 1846**
Northram
Hertfordshire

My dear Madam,

Your letter announcing the melancholy news of the loss of your father that you have sustained, came upon me most unexpected. Even at your fathers advanced age, it still comes as a sad loss for you to have a sudden bereavement which you undergo. I fully comprehend the distress of your feelings and I beg you that I will fully participate in them with you.

Believe me, W. W. Hope.

Rayson ***Paris 14th Feb 1846***
Gamekeeper
Rushton.

Rayson,

In my quarterly accounts, I find £15 charged to me for damage done by game to the land of Jarvis for his crop loss. Your disobedience of my orders to kill all the game was not as I desired. I have therefore instructed Brunning to settle the account with Jarvis and pay you all wages due to date as I have no further need for your services.

Signed for W. W. Hope.

Reverend J Wetherall **Paris 16th February 1846**

My dear Sir,

Your letter of the 16th, which I received today, has rather embarrassed me, and to cut the matter short, I have directed Brunning to come over directly and I will settle the matter with him what course I shall adopt. I have directed him to call on you to get all the information he can and a few hours conservation with him will enable me, I think, to come directly to a final determination and I beg you will believe that it has always been and will be a great satisfaction to myself, to send you any of the little courtesies of life, such as shooting etc and I always feel particularly happy in being able thus to expose the whole family to such gifts. This is the foundation of friendships.

My health, thank god, is very good this winter and I received great benefit from my stay at Wisisbaden. My rheumatism is what the doctor calls acute rheumatism and has been very painful, so the waters were a sovereign remedy for it. As I suffer a lot from it, I shall go back there again in the summer and then I shall come to visit you at Rushton and find your thoughts on the nasty railroad. It pains me a lot that I do not find time to spend at Rushton, as it is a place I love, as it reminds me of the place of my childhood.

Give my complements to Mrs Wetherall with my great esteem.

Believe me, W. W. Hope.

Mr Westerman ***Paris 18th April 1846***

Sir,

I have the honour of sending you the linen order that I have promised to despatch to you. If you have any observations to make to me on this matter, you will find me here on Monday until 2:00 and Tuesday until 4:00. If there is nothing else to do, I would ask you to send me the exact price of all these items when you return home, so that I can pay the total amount of this order and when you can get the money from various people who have ordered the goods. As I am paying it, I understood that you will tell me the total that I owe. Please tell me also, what method of payment you prefer. If you have a bank in Paris where I can pay, or if you will draw it from my account?

- *A piece of cloth No. 120 of thirty (annes)* for hankerchiefs*
- *Three pieces of thirty annes for curtains No. 80*
- *Two pieces of thirty annes for shirts No. 110*
- *Two tablecloths and twenty-four towels No. 180 for twelve people*
- *Two sets of table linen for twelve people No. 235*
- *Two sets of table linen for twelve people No. 215*
- *Two tea tablecloths at sixty-six francs each, and thirty-six hand towels. N.B. I would ask you to send me the numbers of these as I do not have them.*
- *Twenty-four open serviettes No. 215*
- *Six tablecloths No. 220 for design, No. 305 for quality. They must be two square annes.*
- *A large tablecloth of eight and a quarter annes in length, by three and a quarter annes. Design No. 215, Quality No. 245*
- *Two tablecloths and twenty-four serviettes, two annes by three. No. 260*
- *Four two annes bands, Four one anne bands, Four three anne bands, Four one and a half anne bands*
- *Eight sets of towels of thirty annes, No. 285*
- *One set of No. 120*
- *Two sets of No. 110*

** This letter was translated from French. The translator did not know what the word *anne* meant, as none of the dictionaries contained it, but the translator presumed it to be a small measurement.*

Messrs Freshfield ***Paris 11th April 1846***

Gentlemen,

It is now many months since my steward Brunning put papers in to your hands relating to the exchange of lands with the church. I feel that you should have finished the matter by now. While I feel anxious to do business with you, I feel that I may have to terminate it, unless you finish as soon as possible, so I would be obliged if you would reply just what you intend doing with the matter.

Signed for W. W. H.

Mr Crosby **Paris August 1846**

In reply to come of your questions, I have got a recipe for paint stripper and as soon as I have got it translated, I will send it to you for Brunning. Tell him to sell most of the fat sheep this season.

To place iron bars at all lower windows which have no shutters at the Hall. They are to be fitted on the inside and not on the outside, this is much safer.

Put a temporary fence along the wall of the area where your counting house is to be placed. I do not think that the Hall is well protected at night, so I request that you find confidential servants to live in another part of the hall that is occupied by Brunning and his family. The fence build must be the best, but cheapest and of common construction.

The weather has been so hot in Paris that people are sleeping outside with no clothing on. I have never known it so hot.
Believe me, W. W. Hope.

Mr Crosby **October 1846**

Send hampers of game with them empty and ask Birmingham to find out what the charges are to be from London to Dover and Calais or packet from London to Calais.

Mr Brunning ***Paris December 1846***

Mr Hope thinks that if ever he had a thorn in his side as Mr Hamborough has, if Mr Hope wanted to extract it, he would have to pay its weight in gold, as it has always been the case with him. He does not wish to harm Mr Hamborough, but as this gentleman wants to be accommodating, Mr Hope in return would wish to be accommodated. Also, Mr Hambrough wishes for one thing, Ashers farm house. Mr Hope in return would wish to have that lot of land which belongs to Mr Hamborough and is surrounded by those fields belonging to Mr Hope and marked on the map:
9-1..9-3...9-5...9-6.. 9-7...9-8... 9-9...9-10, at a valuation that would be fair to both parties and Mr Hope would be willing to pay the difference. This is Mr Hopes idea and he will leave it to you to make the best bargain you can. Not forgetting that Mr Hamborough has a terrible thorn that he ought to pay for.

Signed for, W. W. Hope.

Mr John Hambrough Esq **Paris 5th December 1846**
Steephill Castle
Isle of Wight

Sir,

I yesterday received your letter. You did me the honour of addressing it to myself from Steephill Castle. In answer to its contents, I beg you to refer you to my agent Mr Brunning who resides at Rushton hall, who has my entire confidence, as well as the management of all my landed properties in England. Please direct your agent to address him and I have no doubt that they will come to a final decision, which I will be happy to ratify.

Believe me, W. W. Hope.

Mr Brunning ***Paris 22nd December 1846***

Sir,

The last hamper of game arrived here well. You will need some vegetable seeds for the new kitchen gardens, Cardoons and beetroot are suitable.

Mr H. says his health is not sufficiently good enough for him to undergo the journey to Calais to meet you, he will send secure directions on the best route here. Has the keeper got the new gun?

Signed for, W. W. H.

Chapter 9

January to December 1847

The south side of Rushton Hall as Hope built it

Mr Hooper ***Paris 20th January 1847***
Haymarket.

Sir,

Your letter of the 18th, I do not understand you. A very large roomy, and easy barouche for the town is easy work for two 17 hand horses. Find me a drawing of what you think best.

Signed for, W. W. H.

Mr Hooper ***Paris 23rd January 1847***

I think that you misunderstood my last letter of the 15th. Therein I stated: The travelling carriage you are building for me will have a water closet that will work well. I therefore beg you to suspend the building of the carriage till such times as you can report favourably on the subject. Should the water closet not work well, the carriage will remain on your hands.

Signed for, W. W. H.

P. S. If you send me the drawings of the water closet, I can then inform you of any changes that might be an improvement.

Mr Brunning ***Paris 26th January 1847***

Sir,

The game and mutton arrived here in good condition. Mr Hope has requested me to inform you that you have to go to Calais to meet him there and that you are to bring with you the Russian obligations as ordered in my letter of the 16th of January. I shall write to you again tomorrow, but it could be on Wednesday or Thursday as am so busy.

Signed for, W. W. H.

Brunning ***Paris 27th January 1847***

Mr Hope will be at Calais and Mr hope requests me likewise to say to you that he wishes for you to take a trustworthy person with you as far as Dover for safety sake, as you bring such a large package. The most confidential man and the most useful would be old John. You will have to give him some money to get back to Rushton.

When you leave Rushton with old John, go direct to my London house for the packet, then you with john will take a cab to the insurance office where you will do business. When you finish, go by the first train to Dover, where you and John will sleep at the Ship inn and be able to cross on the next morning packet, the English mail. As soon as you are safely on board with the packet for me, John will then return to Rushton. I think that is the best and safest way

Signed for, W. W. H.

Mr Hooper
Haymarket.

Sir,

Referring to my last letter of the 23rd, I requested that the water closet may be on the left hand side of the carriage, or middle, whatever was the best, but on no account have it on the right side. Give as much room inside the carriage as you can in height and breath and do not build too low and the axles should be same width, as the carriage has to go over very bad roads and ruts. With regards to the Barouche, you may build it according to the plans you think best. Take great care that it hangs level when the coachman's box is with or without a person on it. Let it be smart. I will need the Barouche finished by April.

Signed for, W.W. H.

Mr Brunning. ***Paris 15th February 1847***

Please forward the enclosed bill to Mr Freshfield. Mr Hope desires that you should pay it when you go up to town. Next time you are in town, call to see Mr Hooper to find how the work is on the travelling coach. Mr Hooper might need advice on how the water closet should be fitted. Please report at once what you find out.

Mr Hope says that I am to inform you that you must take respecting expenses for your board and lodging whenever you go from Rushton. Mr Hope thinks ten shillings a day should be sufficient and Mr hope will pay for the coach train and packet boat, but keep a accurate record of accounts.

Signed for, W. W. H.

Mr Ferdinand St John **Paris 24th February 1847**

My dear Sir,

I will propose you as a temporary member of the club with the greatest of pleasure, but I must tell you that I am very unpopular with the old wigs, who are convinced that I was the cause of various alterations, with regard to the dining and smoking department. I have resigned from being a member of that committee, which did not prevent the last person from having fifty-seven black balls.

Mr Cope is popular there. It might help for you if I have a word, as it only requires a little word from a committee member. Nevertheless, I will run the risk, so I am at your disposal.

Believe me W. W. Hope.

Mr Brunning **Paris 25th February 1847**

Has the situation for a clerk been filled? Remember the last one you had turned up drunk and you sent him back on the next train to London. I do not think you will do better than to have Jenkins to be clerk.

Have you heard from the Midland railway and have you succeeded in getting them to put a carriage halt or station at Rushton, in or near the village?

Believe me W.W. Hope

Messrs Hooper ***Paris 27th February 1847***

I have received your letter this morning and one from my steward. He tells me that he had not been able to see the water closet. As he is perfectly competent to judge of this, you would do well to take his opinion. You seem to be putting the cart before the horse in building the carriage first, then the water closet afterwards. I will repeat it, that if the water closet does not suit me, I shall leave the carriage in your hands. Take particular care that there is no name anywhere on the carriages. I shall then be able to get them in to France without paying duty.

There should be a movable separation inside and a table that can be pulled up when not in use. I do not think you understood about the imperials. Send me what you intended doing - your explanation. I think you also misunderstood when I said five springs. That was to include the crop springs under the carriage similar to the ones behind. The little carriage you made for me some time ago, the leather block in the middle of the spring area was so badly frayed that I was obliged to have it repaired here.

The barouche must be ready by April 15th. Paint the barouche in green, picked out in white. You must arrange so as to put an old box on the front and back, so that it will not injure the carriage, but make it look well used, so that I can get it past customs duty free.

The travelling carriage, painted in olive green, lined in dark green and white with silver fittings, no arms or crest. I will have to get them done in Paris, as I must get to a wedding in France, but do not wish to pay duty on a new Carriage.

Signed for, W. W. H.

Mr Hooper ***Paris 2nd March 1847***

I wrote to you yesterday about the colour of the carriage. On the travelling carriage I desire to have good strong locks, very simple, all to open with one key, very simple, no nonsense. I beg you will let my steward explain to you my ideas on the subject, as he knows what mean.

Signed for, W. W. H.

Mr Hooper ***Paris 3rd March 1847***

You must pay attention to the guard rail, which is to replace the hind imperial. This must be made to look like an Imperial and also be movable at leisure, with the leather at the top (which is to cover what goes underneath) and be ample. My steward could not see the water closet as you had not started work on it when he called in. Work must be finished on the barouche by April 15th this year. I gave you the order soon enough.

Signed for, W. W. H.

Mr Hooper ***Paris 14th April 1847***

I have received your letter of the 12th and I am very annoyed that my carriage will not be ready before the first week in May. I told you back in January that I wanted the barouche by the end of April. You have been very negligent, as you have had plenty and favourable weather. It's of no use giving me your time for building a carriage, as the more time you have, the longer the delay.

Signed for, W. W. H.

233

Vous m'avisez en outre une vente de 11. obligations Russes en date du 7 Ct (sans désignation de Numéros) laquelle a produit net £ 11669. 17. dont vous m'avez crédité

Si ainsi que vous me le mandez la baisse ~~[illegible]~~ sur les places de Londres et Paris a arrêté les transactions sur votre marché, d'un autre côté je vois avec plaisir qu'elle n'a pas affecté la valeur de nos obligations russes qui restent cotées à de bons prix —

Veuillez agréer &c WWH

Sir, Paris April 14th 1847

I have received your letter of the 12th inst. and am very much annoyed that my carriage will not be ready before the first week in May. In my letter of the 29th January I wrote you I should want the Barouche by the end of April. You have been very negligent as you have had plenty of time & very favourable weather. It is of no use giving you time for building a carriage, as the more time you have the longer you delay. &c. WWH

Reçu de Mr E. Loyseau agent de change, la somme de Dix mille francs à porter au débit de mon compte

Paris le 15 avril 1847.

B. F. 10000.

WWH —

A copy of a page from the original book

Mr Brunning ***Paris 29th April 1847***

Mr Hope desires that iron shutters are to be fitted for all the lower parts of the house. Send Mr Hope details of all the wallpapers for the interior and likewise from the garret.

Mr Hope wishes you to inform Messrs Harman that they and the Bank of England spelt his title wrong. It should read William Williams Hope of the Manor of Trevorrack. Check that they get it correct on any deeds and then take the deeds to Rushton and keep them with Mr Hopes other papers.

Signed for, W. W. H.

Mr Brunning ***Paris 28th May 1847***

Sir,

Mr Hope has requested me to say that he did not see you mention in your letters anything of dogs. What of the dog that was to be brought up properly and broken in for himself? Mr Hope says that the railroad has given up for the time being, so his interests in shooting will be protected for another season. Therefore you can breed and rear as much game as possible.

The sporting dogs Mr Hope says you may keep are a pointer, although Mr Hope thinks with the exception of a three week season, most dogs are unnecessary and therefore Mr Hope says keep at Rushton three spaniels, two retrievers and if you can find one good setter that will do no harm to the game, but young dogs. Mr Hope considers that most young dogs are useless and better to have none at all than them, so until they are thoroughly broken and perfect in command, Mr Hope does not wish to see them.

Mr Hope says give the workmen a shilling or sixpence if they find any pieces of art work or treasure when working at the Hall amongst the rubbish. Mr Puckford by those means picked up very near one hundred old coins.

Have you discovered who informed on someone for shooting without a licence?

Signed for, W. W. H.

Mr Hooper ***Paris 10th June 1847***

Sir,

I request that the travelling coach be made ready by July 1st. Mr Dessin of the hotel Dessin, Calais, had undertaken to have my carriage brought over in his name, so to avoid duty on it as it will be called his in name. I will send him the order and the name of persons who will be with it. Let me know their names, so that I can forward the information to him.

Signed for, W. W. H.

Mr Dessin ***Paris 10th June 1847***
Hotel Dessin

Mr Dessin Sir,

Mr Hope will be sending his man Martins to Calais with a letter and some money for you. A carriage will come to you from England that will be in your name. Mr Birmingham will come with it.

Signed for, W. W. H.

Mr Birmingham ***Paris 18th July 1847***
13 Berkeley Square

Mr Birmingham Sir,

The trunks that you were to forward have not yet arrived here in Paris. The carriage arrived here on Wednesday, but no trunks and Mr Dessin says the fault lies with you for their loss. So I have sent a man to Boulogne to see if he can discover them. Pray send them, as such negligence is unpardonable on your part, and on the part of those you employ. Here I am waiting for those cursed trunks, which you should have sent properly, but failed to do so.
I was to commence my journey the day the coach arrived. It was Wednesday and today is Thursday, still no trunks and I just have to start on Friday. All this is due to your negligence in every thing you do. You also forgot to forward the keys to the trunks.
Also the beer you sent the other day took a full fortnight to go between Dover and Calais.

Signed for, W. W. H.

Mr Crosby ***Paris 7th April 1847***
1 East Brook Place
Castle Street
Dover .

Mr Crosby,

Show Brunning the enclosed papers, which I hope that they are right. Tell Brunning not to make a public sale of Rushton, but put it in the hands of some agents. They must only send people to look that are really interested and want to buy. This way Brunning will get the best price out of them he can. I want to give my power of attorney to Mr John Brunning of Rushton Hall.

Signed for, W. W. H.

Miss Maunsell **Wiesbaden 12th July 1847**
Thorpe Malsor

Dear Madam,

It is with the greatest astonishment that I received your letter yesterday, with your complaints against Brunning. During the number of years he has been in my service, I have never received any complaints against him. I am always being praised for his conduct by everybody and I am told that good fortune provides me with such an excellent steward. I know him as a very kind hearted man, but firm, with my interests at stake. I think you and your family must have an imbibed an undue prejudice against him and therefore, I suppose you have judged under that influence.

I have laid out a great deal of money in improving the grounds at Rushton. I was there three weeks ago and told Brunning not to let dogs or horses in the park, as they will damage the turfs. All have been new laid. It came as no surprise to me when I was told some area had been damaged by horse's hoofs and not of his making.

I think therefore, but with all deference, as I have the honour of addressing a lady, that you did not show Mr Brunning the indulgence he is entitled to, considering he has a great responsibility. He has not written to me, as I never tell where I am. Rushton is certainly not in a fit state to ride in at present. Should you wish to make a visit, then go to the main gate and ask the porter if it is suitable to see, but on no account let my dogs out, as I dislike them running about the park.

I have to request your indulgence, for this letter is written at a time when I am still suffering from illness and fatigue and for the last few months, life and property has been in great danger and almost every day I deplore the loss of valuable friends, which makes things at Rushton all seen so very trivial.

Give my kindest remembrances to your father and mother.

Believe me, W. W. Hope.

The reminiscences and recollections of the notabilities of Captain Gronow

Taken from the notabilities of London and Paris 1810-1860

Mr Williams Hope and his Mistress - This gentleman inherited on coming of age a fortune of £40,000 sterling a year from his reputed father, a Dutchman. He exhibits alternately extreme recklessness in expenditure and the stinginess of a miser.

He would one day spend thousands of pounds on a ball or supper, and then keep his servants for days on cold meat and stale bread. His mistress, Mlle Jenny Coulon, a charming actress told me that Mr Hope, suspecting her of infidelity, breakfasted with her at her lodgings as if nothing had occurred, and on leaving said, "Oh, my dear, I wish you would give me your diamonds, that I may have them newly set". Jenny never imagined that her lover had the remotest idea of playing her false, readily gave them to him, and a fortnight afterwards he returned the ornaments, expressing a hope that she would be pleased with the setting. On the following day, what was Jenny's horror as receiving a visit from the jeweller, who called upon her with a bill it for "taking out the diamonds and replacing them with paste". The enraged fair one applied to the police for redress, but found she had no remedy, having voluntarily relinquished all claim on the diamonds by giving them up to the donor. Yet this man has been known to portion the daughter of a lady of rank with £20,000.

Melancholy result of a ball-At one of Mr William Hope's balls, the crowd of visitors was so great, that many persons were obliged on leaving the saloon to take shelter under an archway until the arrival of their carriages. The wind, a keen northeaster, was the cause of a sore throat and a fever to many of the fair visitors; and of those present, a General Didier and his wife, a remarkably hansom couple, were seized with quinsy, and in eight-and-forty hours afterwards they both died, and were carried to their last resting-place at Père La Chaise, Nantes. This lamentable event created an unusual sensation in Paris at the time, and was the theme of conversation in every quarter.

When it was mentioned to a friend of mine, he coolly observed that he pitied the lady, but not the General, for it was glorious end for a soldier to be killed by a ball.

How to get invited to a ball - Mr Williams Hope's large fortune enabled him to give the most splendid entertainments to the *beau monde* of Paris. At his balls and parties all the notables of the city were to be seen, and no expense was spared to make them the most sumptuous entertainments then given. It was his custom, when the invitations were issued, not to open any letters till the party was over; to save him the mortification of refusing those who had not been invited.

It happened that a certain Marquis, well in Paris, who had married the sister of a prince, was desirous of being present at one of these assemblies, and according wrote, requesting the favour of an invitation for himself, his wife, and his wife's sister, the Princess de C*. Receiving no answer, the Marquis called upon Mr Hope, who received him with his usual courtesy.

The Marquis began by expressing his surprise that his letter had remained unanswered, when Mr Hope assured him that he had not received the letter in question; explaining the custom before alluded to. This explanation, however, did not satisfy the Marquis, who observed that such a proceeding was, to say the least of it, extraordinary, as letters were generally written in expectation of their receiving an answer with the least possible delay; and he added, "Mr Hope, by your conduct you have not only insulted me, my wife, and sister-in-law, but several of my friends. I must therefore tell you, that the fist time I meet you in the Champs Elysées or the Bois de Boulogne, I will give order to my coachman to drive against your carriage; which insult you will naturally resent". Mr Hope replied "I am not of your opinion as to the necessity of having my carriage injured through the awkwardness or stupidity of your coachman; and to avoid all further altercation, I will have the honour to send you as many cards of invitation to my ball as you may wish for yourself and friends".

The Marquis swallowed the bait, returned to his wife, overcame the objections as to the manner in which the *entrée* was obtained, and appeared with her and his sister-in-law on the appointed evening. They were received with due honours, and when supper was announced, Mr Hope advanced towards the princess, and offering her his arm, conducted her to the page of honour at his right hand at the supper-table.

The rank of the Marquis and his sister-in-law had probably more influence than his threat in procuring for him the invitation, as the vanity and ostentation of Mr Hope were no less remarkable than his meanness and eccentricity.

**It is presumed that the whole name has been omitted to protect the identity.*

(Also found in Captain Gronow's book)

Many people in Europe have the Teinge or Scauld-Head a very loathsome complaint. Many Englishman here in Paris do not take their hats off when they meet ladies /lady, it is not that the English men in Paris are very rude when they meet a lady, but they keep their hats on so that they may not catch the pest, that most horrible disease that is not known of in England.

William Williams Hope Esquire

This is the last Will & Testament of me William Williams Hope of Rushton in the County of Northamptonshire and of Trevorrick in the County of Cornwall I devise and bequeath all my real and personal Estate whatsoever and wheresoever unto [illegible] of No. 1 East [illegible] Place [illegible] his heirs executors administrators and assigns [illegible] absolutely I appoint John [illegible] of Rushton in the County of Northamptonshire the sole Executor of this my Will and I revoke all former Wills In witness whereof I have hereunto set my hand and seal this fifteenth day of May one thousand eight hundred and fifty one — W. Williams Hope (LS) — Signed sealed published and declared by William Williams Hope of Rushton in the County of Northamptonshire and Trevorrick in the County of Cornwall the testator as his last Will in the presence of us present at the same time and who at his request and in his presence and in the presence of each other have hereunto signed our names as witnesses thereto — Charles Henry Okey [illegible] to Her Majesty's Embassy at Paris — John [illegible] No. 49 Avenue des Champs Elysées Paris [illegible]

This is a Codicil to my Will which is dated the fifteenth day of May one thousand eight hundred and fifty one I give the sum of Twenty thousand pounds [illegible] to [illegible] and the sum of fifteen thousand [illegible] pounds sterling to [illegible] also the sum of five hundred pounds sterling to [illegible] of Rushton and I direct the above named [illegible] to be paid out of the real and personal estate bequeathed in my said Will And I confirm my said Will in all other respects In witness whereof I have hereunto set my hand and seal this thirty first day of May one thousand eight hundred and fifty one — W. Williams Hope (LS) — Signed sealed and published and declared as a Codicil to the last Will by the said William Williams Hope in the presence of us present at the same time and who in his presence and in the presence of each other have hereunto subscribed our names as witnesses thereto — [illegible]

Proved at London with a Codicil [illegible] June 1855 before the Worshipful [illegible] George [illegible] Doctor of Laws and Surrogate by the Oath of John [illegible] the sole Executor to whom Admon was granted having been first sworn duly to admr.

August 29th 1857

COPY OF THE WILL OF WILLIAM WILLIAMS HOPE OF RUSHTON.

This is the last will & testament of me William Williams Hope in the county of Northamptonshire and of Trewrthenick (read as Trevorrick) in the county of Cornwall. I give and request all my soul and personal estate .... And .... unto VINUS HODGEKINSON - CROSBY of No I Brook Place Castle., Dover, His Paris executor absolutely I appoint JOHN BRUNNING of RUSHTON in the county of Northamptonshire the sole executor of my will and revoke all former wills .... Witness, ... my .... seal ....of May One Thousand eight Hundred and Fifty One. W. Williams Hope, signus, scalco puliolus and solario by William Williams Hope of Rushton in the county of Northamptonshire and Trewrthenick in the county of Cornwall this testot as his last will in the presence of witness Charles Henry Cheylounoel of her Majestys Embassy of Paris --- John Piqweed No 49 Avenue De Champes - Elyees Paris, Barrister.

THIS IS A CODICIL to my 'Will which is catalogued fifteenth day of May, One Thousand Eight Hundred & Fifty One · I give the sum of Twenty Thousand Pounds sterling to............of ....of Paris, also the sum of Fifteen Thousand pounds sterling to Mdlle AMELIE CHAMERLAT De ABRAN, of Paris. Also the sum of five thousand pounds sterling to MARIASARGENT of Rushton (spinster) and, PAID OUT OF the ......and personal estate ......in my said will .... My said will ..., order .... Of my ....this the thirty first day of May One thousand Eight hundred and fifty five

W. Williams Hope. Signos Sealos & Publiolus as a codocil to a ... & will by the vaio William Williams Hope in the prosouire of......... at the .... and .... his proucurious in the prosure of .... as .... Cpt ...., ASHBY, RUSHTON to B S....ver Rushton.

This a translation of a copy of Mr Hope's will:

This is the last testament and will of me William Williams Hope, of Rushton in the county of Northamptonshire and of Trevarrack in the county of Cornwall, I give and bequest all my sole and personal estate to Vinus Hodgekinson Crosby of No 1 Brook Place Dover, my pers*onal executor.*

Dated May 1st 1851.

Codicil to my will Dated May 15th 1851.

I William Williams Hope give Twenty Thousand Pounds to (name I cannot read) of Paris.
I also give to Mdlle Amelie Chamerlet De Sabran of Paris the sum of Fifteen Thousand Pounds.
I also give to Maria Sargent (spinster) of Rushton the sum of Five Thousand Pounds.

W. W. Hope.

Note: Maria Sargent was the niece of John Brunning, steward of the Rushton Estate. Maria lived at the Hall with Mr & Mrs Brunning and she came with them from Suffolk in 1831.

The Obituary of W. W. Hope

On the 21st of January 1855, William Williams Hope was found dead in his bed at his home at the Grand Hotel he built in Paris at 121 Rue Dominique, Faubourg St Germain.

He detested male society and formed a coterie of ladies, distinguished for their musical and artistic capabilities. On his death they were left large legacies. He possessed a large collection of diamonds, many of which he wore on his person. He would never meet his dinner guests before the dinner and then he would make a grand entrance showing off his diamonds, which included a famous Black Diamond.

Mr Hope, never married, but in his will he left a large sum to Mr. V.H. Crosby, stocks and shares to Mr Brunning and five thousand pounds to the niece of Mr Brunning, Maria Sargent. His lady friend for eighteen years Miss De Sabran had his horses and carriages, but Miss De Sabran said that they were not his to leave to her. A great court case then followed and the court decided that she could have the use of them in the day only, and not at night. He left behind a vast collection of curiosities and gems, the Paris sale took several days.

His Rushton Hall estate was sold to Miss Thornhill and at his sale, which took ten days, Miss Thornhill bought a lot of the house fittings and furniture that was in the hall. Mr Hope had bought the Rushton Estate in 1928 for £140,000, after his death it was sold for £165,000.

Mr Hope had spent a lot of money on rebuilding the Hall after part was destroyed by fire in 1835. Most of the grand Rushton Hall we see today was rebuilt by William Williams Hope. He was High Sheriff for Northamptonshire in 1832. He seldom came to his Northamptonshire home, but came for the shooting. Mr Hope also had estates and mines in Cornwall and lands in Leicestershire.

Hope

CATALOGUE OF

THE VALUABLE EFFECTS

AT

RUSHTON HALL

NORTHAMPTONSHIRE.

RUSHTON HALL, NORTHAMPTONSHIRE.

A Catalogue

OF

THE CONTENTS OF

THE NOBLE MANSION

OF THE LATE

W. WILLIAMS HOPE, ESQ.,

RUSHTON HALL, NORTHAMPTONSHIRE,

Four Miles from Kettering, Twelve from Wellingborough, and Sixteen from Northampton,

COMPRISING THE

ELEGANT PARISIAN FURNITURE,

Wardrobes of Bed and Table Linen,

PLATED ARTICLES, CHINA, GLASS, &c.

A Fine Collection of

PICTURES, BRONZES, AND ANTIQUES,

OF GREAT RARITY;

CELLAR OF CHOICE WINES;

A Fine Musical Library, and Collection of Literary Works,

OF THE PRINCIPAL ENGLISH AND FRENCH AUTHORS.

LIVE AND DEAD FARMING STOCK;

WHICH WILL BE SOLD BY AUCTION BY

MR. C. WARTON,

ON THE PREMISES,

ON MONDAY, THE 6TH OF AUGUST, 1855,

AND SEVERAL FOLLOWING DAYS, AT ELEVEN FOR TWELVE O'CLOCK EACH DAY.

May be Viewed on Friday and Saturday previous to the Sale, and Catalogues had (1*s.* each) at Hope's Arms, Rushton; Royal Hotel, Kettering; the Angel, Market Harborough; the Royal Hotel, Rugby; the Bell, Leicester; Angel, Peterborough; George Hotel, Northampton; the Hind, Wellingborough; Swan, Bedford; of **Messrs. ROWLAND and HACON, Solicitors, No. 31, Fenchurch Street;** and of

Mr. C. WARTON, Auctioneer and Estate Agent, No. 7, Union Court, Old Broad Street, Removed from Threadneedle Street.

NOTE.—*A Private View by Cards only, on Wednesday and Thursday previous to the Sale.*

ORDER OF SALE.

RUSHTON HALL, NEAR KETTERING, NORTHAMPTONSHIRE.

FIRST DAY'S SALE, on Monday, 6th August, 1855.

THE FURNITURE OF NINE BED AND DRESSING ROOMS—THE SOUTH FRONT PARLOUR—AND PORTION OF THE LINEN.

SECOND DAY'S SALE, Tuesday, 7th August.

THE FURNITURE OF BATH ROOM AND BED ROOM—SIX BED AND DRESSING ROOMS—GENTLEMAN'S ROOM—INNER HALL—AND PORTION OF THE LINEN.

THIRD DAY'S SALE, Wednesday, 8th August.

THE COLLECTION OF PICTURES, ENAMELS, BRONZES, &c.

FOURTH DAY'S SALE, Thursday, 9th August.

THE FURNITURE OF FIVE BED AND DRESSING ROOMS—THE DINING ROOM—GRAND HALL—LIBRARY—AND THE PLATED ARTICLES.

FIFTH DAY'S SALE, Friday, 10th August.

THE LIBRARY OF BOOKS.

SIXTH DAY'S SALE, Monday, 13th August.

THE FURNITURE OF SEVERAL PRINCIPAL AND SECONDARY BED ROOMS—PICTURE FRAMES—AND PORTION OF THE LINEN.

SEVENTH DAY'S SALE, Tuesday, 14th August.

THE FURNITURE OF THE PRINCIPAL AND TWO OTHER BED ROOMS AND THE DRAWING ROOM—ALSO THE LIBRARY OF MUSICAL WORKS.

EIGHTH DAY'S SALE, Wednesday, 15th August.

THE CELLAR OF CHOICE WINES—THE FOWLING PIECES, GUNS, AND SWORDS—GARDEN PLANTS—SWANS, BOATS, &c.

NINTH DAY'S SALE, Thursday, 16th August.

THE FURNITURE OF LINEN ROOM—SEVERAL BED ROOMS—HALL—PORTION OF THE LINEN—SERVICES OF CUT GLASS AND CHINA—AND FRENCH COOKERY UTENSILS.

TENTH DAY'S SALE, Friday, 17th August.

THE FURNITURE IN BAILIFF'S HOUSE IN THE PARK—THE BROOD MARES AND COLTS—THE LIVE AND DEAD FARMING STOCK—AND THE MATERIALS, &c., IN OUT-BUILDINGS.

NOTE—The Sale will commence at Eleven for Twelve o'Clock punctually each day (except Wednesday the 8th); and Lots will be delivered between the hours of Nine and Eleven on the day.

On Friday and Saturday the 10th and 11th August, the delivery of Furniture will go on between the hours of Nine and Five.

NOTE.—Trains leave the Euston Square Station for Northampton and Wellingborough, from which places conveyances may be obtained.

CONDITIONS OF SALE.

1. *The highest bidder to be the buyer, and if any dispute arise between two or more bidders, the lot in dispute shall be immediately put up again and re-sold.*

2. *No person to advance less than One Shilling at each bidding; Five Shillings above five pounds; and so on in proportion.*

3. *The purchasers are, if required, positively to pay down a deposit of Five Shillings in the Pound on each lot, and give in their names and places of abode, in default of which the lot shall be put up again and re-sold, and such defaulter's bidding will not be taken again.*

4. *The remainder of the purchase-money to be paid and the lots taken away, with all faults, at the buyer's expense before the* 23*rd of August,* 1855, *and in default of this the auctioneer will not be responsible for loss or damage to any lots remaining, the sole risk being with the purchaser, who shall pay for a man's time attending to deliver (over and above the time allowed), at* 5s. *per day, or the lots may be forfeited at the option of the auctioneer.*

5. *Any allowance claimed for deficiences to be calculated by the auctioneer, in proportion to the purchase-money given, and in no case to be subject to other estimates or after sales, and no allowance will be made at all for errors of description, or for presumed deficiences, after the lots are once delivered to the purchaser.*

Lastly,—Upon failure of complying with the above conditions, the money deposited in part payment shall be forfeited, the lot or lots remaining uncleared after the time specified, shall be re-sold by public or private sale, and the deficiency (if any) by such second sale, together with all charges attending the same, shall be made good by the defaulter or defaulters at this present sale.

FIRST DAY'S SALE,

AT RUSHTON HALL, NEAR KETTERING, NORTHAMPTONSHIRE,

ON MONDAY, 6TH AUGUST, 1855,

Commencing at Eleven for Twelve precisely.

No. 26, MAID-SERVANTS' BEDROOM.

LOT
1 A painted iron bedstead
2 A palliasse
3 A wool mattress
4 A feather bed, bolster, and pillow
5 Three blankets and coverlid
6 A painted iron bedstead
7 A palliasse
8 A wool mattress
9 A feather bolster and 2 pillows
10 Four blankets and coverlid
11 Two pieces of bedside carpet, and 3 rush-seat chairs
12 A japanned corner washstand and fittings
13 Two small dressing glasses
14 A painted dressing table and towel horse
15 A painted wardrobe, with shelves, and drawers under
16 Sundries

No. 27, STORE ROOM.

17 pieces of Brussels carpeting, yards
18 Four sheepskin rugs
19 About 30 yards of Scotch stair carpet
20 Thirty-five yards of stair drugget
21 A counterpane
22 Three hair bolsters
23 A French canopy bedstead
24 A panelled door and a high linen basket
25 Four gilt picture frames, glazed
26 A small pier glass and leather travelling trunk

B

FIRST DAY'S SALE.

No. 28, SERVANT'S ROOM.

LOT
27 A steel mounted fender, set of fire irons, guard, and piece of Kiddermnster carpet
28 A japanned French bedstead
29 A palliasse
30 A wool mattress
31 Feather bed, bolster and pillow, a white counterpane and a coloured ditto
32 Four blankets
33 A wainscot chest of five drawers
34 A painted dressing table, ditto towel horse, and a small glass
35 A mahogany corner washstand and fittings, and 2 cane seat chairs

No. 29, FRONT BED ROOM.

36 A brass mounted high wire fender and fire irons
37 A Kidderminster carpet, about 20 yards
38 Japanned dressing table and four matted chairs
39 Ditto ditto and towel horse
40 Ditto washstand and fittings
41 Ditto ditto
42 A mahogany inlaid French bidet and pan
43 A mahogany slab frame swing dressing glass and mahogany towel horse
44 A wainscot chest of five drawers

No. 30, WEST FRONT ROOM.

45 A brass mounted fender and set of fire irons
46 A 3 ft. painted iron tent bedstead
47 A hair mattress
48 A wool ditto
49 A feather bed, bolster and pillow
50 A white counterpane and 4 blankets
51 A 3 feet 6 inch painted iron tent bedstead
52 A hair mattress
53 A wool ditto
54 A Feather bed, bolster and pillow
55 Four blankets and a counterpane

FIRST DAY'S SALE.

LOT

56 A Kidderminster carpet, 15 yards, and a piece yard wide ditto, 5 yards

57 A wainscot chest of 5 drawers

58 A painted wainscot dressing table with drawers, and a japanned washstand and fittings

59 A ditto and ditto

60 A swing dressing glass in mahogany slab frame

61 Two towel horses and 3 matted chairs

FIRST FLOOR.

No. 32, WEST FRONT BED & DRESSING ROOM.

62 A brass mounted fender, set of fire irons, a wire guard, and boot jack

63 A Kidderminster carpet, planned to both rooms, about 24 yards

64 A ditto hearth rug

65 A ditto and a japanned coal receiver

66 A French clock in bronze, with bust ornament

67 A chimney glass, gilt frame, 42 inches by 36

68 A polished mahogany French bedstead, with canopy and new chintz furniture, lined, and fringed

69 Holland covering over ditto

70 A Palliasse

71 A wool mattress

72 A hair ditto

73 A bordered goose feather bed, bolster, and pillow

74 A blanket and a sheet

75 Six polished mahogany chairs, seats stuffed in blue stripe tabaret

76 A mahogany easy chair, stuffed with horse hair, loose seat, and chintz cover

77 A pair of new chintz curtains for bay window, with deep yellow valens, lined with blue, brass rods, bands, and rings

78 An inlaid mahogany Wardrobe, with 3 trays and 3 drawers, folding pannel doors

79 A mahogany pedestal library table, with drawer and green cloth top

80 A mahogany washstand with 2 drawers veined, marble top, drab and green fittings

81 A mahogany dressing table, a ditto towel horse

B 2

FIRST DAY'S SALE.

No. 33, WEST FRONT BED & DRESSING ROOMS.

LOT

82 A brass mounted fender, set of fire irons, and guard
83 A japanned coal scuttle and a small hearth rug
84 A Kidderminster carpet to two rooms, 25 yards
85 A ditto hearth rug
86 A ditto ditto
87 A polished mahogany French bedstead, with canopy top, buff chintz furniture lined
88 A Holland covering
89 A palliasse
90 A hair mattress
91 A ditto bordered
92 A wool ditto
93 A ditto ditto
94 A ditto ditto
95 A bordered goose feather bed, bolster, and pillow
96 Three blankets
97 A Marseilles quilt
98 A mahogany pedestal library table, with drawer, top covered in green morocco
99 An inlaid mahogany Secretary, with folding panelled doors, handsome marble top and fittings
100 Three carved rosewood chairs, seats stuffed with horse hair, in red morocco
101 A mahogany frame easy chair, chintz cover
102 A mahogany tray top table, three drawers
103 A mahogany slab frame swing dressing glass
104 A Parisian clock in bronze relievo and glass shade
105 A pier glass in gilt frame, plate 42 by 34 inches
106 A pair of curtains to large bay window, to match bed furniture
107 A Holland covering
108 A brass mounted fender and a japanned coal scuttle
109 A mahogany washstand, veined marble top, drab and green fittings
110 A mahogany bidet and pan
111 A mahogany boot and shoe stand

FIRST DAY'S SALE.

No. 34, ROOM ADJOINING.

LOT

112 A brass mounted fender and set of fire irons
113 A japanned coal scuttle, wire guard, and boot jack
114 A Kidderminster carpet
115 A ditto hearth rug
116 A ditto ditto
117 Primrose silk furnitnre for a canopy bedstead
118 A Holland covering
119 A pair of window curtains to match bed furniture, with brass poles, rings, and mahogany cornices
120 A palliasse
121 A hair mattress
122 A wool ditto
123 A bordered goose feather bed, bolster, and down pillow
124 Four blankets
125 A Marseilles quilt
126 A silk coverlet lined
127 A mahogany tray top pot cupboard
128 A mahogany pedestal library table with one drawer, top covered with green morocco
129 An inlaid satinwood Bergiere chair, in primrose tabaret, and Holland cover
130 A ditto ditto
131 A French clock in bronze, with figure ornaments and glass shade

No. 35, DRESSING ROOM ADJOINING.

132 A Kidderminster carpet to room, about 20 yards
133 Piece of oil cloth
134 A mahogany bidet and pan
135 Four inlaid maple frame chairs stuffed with hair, covered with primrose silk and Holland covers
136 An inlaid satinwood Bergiere chair, stuffed with hair, in primrose tabaret and Holland cover
137 A ditto ditto

FIRST DAY'S SALE.

LOT

138 A pair of blue silk damask curtains to bay window, with fringe valens, brass bands and rods

139 A mahogany tray top dressing table with two drawers, 3 feet 9 wide

140 A swing dressing glass in mahogany slab frame

141 A mahogany boot and shoe stand

142 A mahogany folding towel horse, foot bath, and jug

143 A mahogany inlaid washstand, with drab and gold fittings

144 A mahogany wardrobe, six shifting trays, and four drawers under, 7 feet 6 by 4 feet

No. 18, SOUTH FRONT PARLOUR.

145 A cast iron fender with standards, set of fire irons, and wire guard

146 A flowered pattern Brussels carpet to room, about 35 yards

147 A hearth rug to match and cover

148 A Holland stair cover and a square Holland cover

149 A japanned and gilt coal vase with cover

150 Six carved and gilt framed chairs, seats and backs stuffed with hair, in crimson and gold satin, and covers

151 Two elbow ditto to match with covers

152 A carved and gilt frame couch *en suite*, with down pillows and cotton cover

153 A pair of elegant rosewood card tables on pillar and claw, lined with crimson cloth, leather cover

154 AN ELEGANT 5 FEET LOO TABLE on carved pillar and claw, *en suite*, and japanned cover

155 A capital mahogany 3 tier dumb waiter on pillar and claw

156 AN ELEGANT FRENCH-POLISHED MAHOGANY SECRETAIRE AND WARDROBE, 3 trays and fittings, marble top, 3 feet wide

157 AN ELEGANT MARQUETRIE WARDROBE, with shelves and drawers under, 3 feet wide, 7 feet high

158 A ditto ditto *en suite*

159 A SQUARE PIANOFORTE in mahogany inlaid case, by Broadwood

160 A rosewood screw music stool

161 A HANDSOME MAHOGANY WINGED BOOK-CASE, with shelves and glazed panelled doors

162 A chimney glass in gilt frame, plate 60 inches by 48 inches

FIRST DAY'S SALE.

LOT

163 A PAIR OF RICH CRIMSON AND GREEN SATIN DAMASK WINDOW CURTAINS, lined with silk, fringe, tassels, and bands, brass cornice, poles and rings, gilt ends, to bay window

164 The Holland covering over ditto

165 Sundries

LINEN.

166 Three pair of fine linen sheets (closet 6)

167 Three pair ditto

168 Three pair ditto

169 Three pair ditto

170 Three pair ditto

171 Three pair ditto

172 Two dozen pillow cases

173 Thirty-two ditto

174 Two large new damask table cloths, 4½ yards long (closet 10)

175 Two ditto

176 Two ditto Huckaback, 4 yards

177 Three diaper ditto, 2½ yards

178 Three ditto

179 Two dozen new table napkins (No. 9)

180 Two dozen ditto

181 Two dozen dusters (No. 10)

182 One dozen knife cloths and two dozen glass cloths

183 Two dozen huckaback towels (No. 9)

184 Two dozen ditto

185 Two dozen ditto

186 Two dozen ditto

187 Two dozen jack towels

188 Two dozen ditto

End of the First Day's Sale.

SECOND DAY'S SALE,

AT RUSHTON HALL, NEAR KETTERING, NORTHAMPTONSHIRE,

ON TUESDAY, 7TH AUGUST, 1855,

Commencing at Eleven for Twelve precisely.

No. 31, BATH ROOM, IN BASEMENT.

LOT
189 A brass mounted fender, set of fire irons and wire guard
190 Piece of Venetian carpet and hearth rug
191 A pier glass in gilt frame
192 About 6 yards Brussels carpet to W. C. passage, and pair of folding steps
193 An arm chair, 2 others, caned seats, and a piece of oilcloth
194 A mahogany towel horse and a circular towel box with cover

SMALL ROOM, *next Bath Room.*

195 A brass mounted fender, set of fire irons, guard and umbrella stand
196 A Venetian carpet
197 A mahogany tray top night convenience
198 A caned elbow chair, 2 gothic chairs, towel horse and boot jack
199 A japanned chest of four drawers
200 A ditto tray top dressing table and dressing glass
201 Ditto washstand with blue fittings
202 A painted iron tent bedstead, with Chintz pattern furniture, lined with blue calico, 3 feet
203 A folding paliasse
204 A bordered wool mattress
205 A feather bed and bolster
206 Four blankets and cotton counterpane

SECOND DAY'S SALE.

No. 19, FRONT DRESSING ROOM.

LOT

206* The Brussels carpet as planned to room, about 15 yards

207 Three pieces of Holland stair cover

208 An inlaid mahogany bidet and pan

209 A towel horse

210 An inlaid pedestal dressing, table with ormoulu ornaments, 2 drawers and framed dressing glass

211 An inlaid mahogany wardrobe with folding doors, 3 feet wide 5 feet 3 in. high

212 A Bergiere chair *ensuite*, stuffed in red damask

213 A circular inlaid mahogany library chair stuffed in scarlet damask

214 Pair of crimson damask window curtains, deep valens, inlaid cornice pole, bands, brass rings, &c., and Holland cover to ditto

215 A blue and white foot bath and large water jug

No. 20, FRONT BED ROOM.

216 A handsome steel polished fender with standards and gilt ornaments, 5 eet.

217 A set of polished steel fire irons with gilt handles

218 A brass wire guard and a japanned coal receiver with cover and handles

219 The handsome Brussels carpet, as planned to room & ante room, about 60 yards and hearth rug to match

220 A Ditto

221 A polished mahogany French canopy bedstead, with crimson damask furniture

222 The Holland covering over ditto

223 A horse hair mattress with cotton cover and a palliasse

224 A wool ditto

225 A goose feather bed, bolster and pillow

226 Two blankets and a sheet

227 Pair of inlaid mahogany Bergiere chairs, in scarlet damask

228 A pair of ditto low backed ditto, *ensuite*

229 Ditto high back Easy Chairs, stuffed with horse hair in scarlet damask, with back cushion

230 A ditto high back Grecian pattern chair in crimson damask

231 A walnut-tree pedestal library table, with 2 drawers, top covered with green cloth, 3 ft. 6 by 2 ft. 6.

232 A rosewood ditto on pillars and claws

233 A mahogany tray top pot cupboard

C

SECOND DAY'S SALE.

LOT

234 An inlaid mahogany wardrobe, with silvered plate glass panels, 3 ft. 6 by 7ft.

235 A Spanish mahogany winged wardrobe, with 4 drawers, trays, and pediment top, 6 feet 6 by 7 feet

236 A rosewood pier table, with carved and gilt scroll legs, plate glass back, and marble top

237 A chimney glass in gilt frame, 72 inches by 54

238 A bronze French clock, with lyre ornaments and glass shade

239 Two pair of crimson damask window curtains, with deep valens, gilt ornaments, rods, &c.

240 The Holland covering over curtains

241 A pair of crimson damask curtains to large bay window, brass cornice, bands, and tassells

242 The Holland covering over ditto

243 The Holland stair covering

ANTE ROOM.

244 Red silk curtains to door

245 Two oak hall chairs

246 Two Ditto

No. 21, SOUTH WEST BED ROOM ADJOINING.

247 A brass mounted fender and fire irons

248 A japanned coal receiver and wire guard

249 Brussels carpet to Room, 5½ yards by 4½

250 A ditto hearth rug

251 A chimney glass in gilt frame, plate 36 inches by 42

252 A Spanish mahogany French canopy bedstead, with poles, &c., chintz pattern furniture, lined with green calico

253 The holland covering over ditto

254 A palliasse

255 A horsehair mattress in linen tick

256 Ditto ditto

257 A wool bed, bolster, and down pillow

258 Two blankets and 1 sheet

259 A mahogany tray top pot cupboard

SECOND DAY'S SALE.

LOT

260 An inlaid mahogany bidet, with fittings

261 Three carved rosewood chairs, seats stuffed in crimson morocco, and covers

262 A Parisian clock in bronze, with bust ornaments and glass shade

263 An easy chair stuffed with hair, cushion and chints cover

264 A CAPITAL SPANISH MAHOGANY WINGED WARDROBE, with 4 drawers and trays, 6 feet wide by 4 feet high

265 A pair of chintz curtains *ensuite*, with mahogany pole, cornice, and brass bands

No. 22, WEST BED ROOM ADJOINING.

266 A high wire brass fender, fire irons, and guard

267 A japanned coal receiver, a wood ditto, and boot jack

268 A chimney glass, in gilt frame, plate 40 inches by 30

269 Brussels carpet to room and dressing-room, about 48 yards

270 A Brussels hearth-rug

271 A Spanish mahogany French bedstead, with canopy, chintz furniture, lined with green, crimson fringe, &c.

272 A palliasse

273 A horse-hair mattress

274 A wool ditto

275 Three blankets and 1 sheet

276 A Marseilles quilt

277 A mahogany tray top pot cupboard

278 Four matted chairs, and a towel horse

279 An easy chair, stuffed with horse-hair, loose seat, and chintz cover

280 A mahogany wardrobe, with 4 drawers, trays, and folding panelled-doors

281 An inlaid card table

282 A pair of chintz curtains to bay window, with valens, to match bed furniture

DRESSING ROOM.

283 A mahogany wash-stand, with 2 drawers—blue fittings

284 A ditto dressing table

8 5 A ditto bidet and pan

286 A ditto swing dressing glass

287 A blue foot-bath and large white jug

288 A chintz curtain and valen to window

C 2

SECOND DAY'S SALE.

No. 23, NORTH-WEST BED ROOM.

LOT

289 A brass-mounted fender and set of fire-irons
290 A Brussels carpet
291 A ditto hearthrug
292 A japanned wash-stand and fittings
293 A mahogany chest of four drawers
294 A swing dressing-glass with two drawers
295 A mahogany towel horse and a chair
296 Twenty-six long brass stair rods and 55 shorter ditto
297 A pair of chintz curtains to match bedstead

No. 24, BED AND DRESSING ROOM.

298 A brass-mounted fender and set of fire-irons
299 Two japanned coal-scuttles, a wire guard, and boot-jack
300 A chimney glass, in gilt frame—plate 36 inches by 42
301 A Brussels carpet to room, about yards
302 A ditto hearthrug
303 Four matted chairs
304 A mahogany French bedstead, with canopy top and pole, chintz furniture, lined
305 A palliasse
306 A wool mattress
307 A ditto bed in striped tick, bolster, and down pillow
308 Three blankets and one sheet
309 A Marseilles quilt
310 A mahogany tray top commode
311 A mahogany chest of 5 drawers
312 A mahogany inlaid card table, lined with green cloth
313 A pair of chintz curtains to bay window
314 One ditto to smaller window
315 A mahogany dressing table with drawer
316 A mahogany frame swing dressing glass, with 2 drawers

SECOND DAY'S SALE.

No. 15, GENTLEMAN'S ROOM.

LOT

317 A steel fender with standards

318 Set of bronze and steel fire irons

319 Brass top fire guard, coal receiver japanned, with cover

320 A coal Receiver with handles

321 Brussels carpet, as planned to room, about 45 yards

322 Ditto hearth rug

323 Pair of green broad cloth curtains to bay window, bordered and figured, with tassels, brass cornice pole and rings

324 AN OCTAGON GLAZED CABINET, in polished oak, on pillar and claw

325 A BEAUTIFUL MARQETRIE SECRETAIRE, WITH ORMOLU ORNAMENTS, DRAWERS AND FITTINGS, AND GALLERY TOP

326 A DITTO SIDEBOARD, with ormolu and enamel ornaments, veined marble top and handsome paw feet

327 AN ELEGANT BUHL AND MAHOGANY WRITING TABLE, with gallery top desk and fittings, covered with green embossed morocco, pair of rich paw feet, also holland cover to ditto

228 A CIRCULAR MAHOGANY LIBRARY CHAIR, with buhl ornaments and pivot seat, paw feet, stuffed in green Morocco *ensuite*, also holland cover

329 SIX MAHOGANY CHAIRS, with stuffed backs and seats in green cloth, buhl ornaments, *ensuite*, also holland covers

330 A MAHOGANY SOFA, with thick horse hair squab in greencloth, holland cover, *ensuite*

331

332 AN ELEGANT HIGH-BACKED LIBRARY CHAIR, of bird's-eye maple wood, with extending frame, stuffed with horse hair in yellow satin damask and holland cover

333 AN ELEGANT MAHOGANY AND BUHL CABINET, richly ornamented, pillar front, pediment top and plate glass panel, 3 feet 6 in. wide, 9 feet 6 in. high

334 A ditto ditto

335 A ditto ditto

336 A ditto ditto

337 A Spanish mahogany loo table with rosewood border, 4 feet diameter

338 A chimney glass in gilt frame, plate 44 in. by 34 in.

SECOND DAY'S SALE.

LOT

339 A PAIR OF ELEGANT ORMOLU CANDELABRAS for 4 lights each, bronze figure and glass shades and stands

340 A CARVED OAK CABINET, with glazed front, shelf lined with crimson damask, pediment stand

341 Two mahogany letter boxes

342 Sundries

INNER HALL.

343 A richly carved and gilt sideboard table, with veined marble top, 3 feet 6

344 A wood basket and cover

345 An oak hat stand with branches

346 Six and two elbow rosewood chairs, crimson leather seats

347 A Palmer's candle lamp ormolu stand

348 A wood basket and a ditto box

349 An inlaid buhl ebonized japanned cabinet, with pediment top and feet, 3 feet wide and 6 feet high

350 Sundries

LINEN.

351 Three pairs of fine linen sheets, No. 6

352 Three pairs of ditto

353 Three pairs of ditto

354 Three pairs of ditto

355 Three pairs of ditto

356 A Marseilles quilt

357 A ditto

358 Three white cotton counterpanes

359 Twelve pillow-cases, 9 toilet covers, and 2 dozen huckaback towels (9)

360 Three dozen huckaback towels

361 Two new damask tablecloths, 4½ yards long (10)

362 Two ditto

363 Two ditto, huckaback, 4 yards

364 Two ditto

365 Two ditto damask, 4 yards

366 Four diaper ditto, 2½ yards

367 Four ditto

THIRD DAY'S SALE,

AT RUSHTON HALL, NEAR KETTERING, NORTHAMPTONSHI

ON WEDNESDAY, 8TH OF AUGUST, 1855,

Commencing at Twelve for One o'Clock precisely.

PAINTINGS AND PRINTS.

LOT		
1	ROTTENHÆMER.........	" The Judgment of Paris,"—with Mercury, &c. (engra by Le Brun)
2	BLARENBURGHE.........	" The Battle of Lanfeldt,"—the chef d'ouvre of this r Master (signed and dated 1768)
3	TERBURG	" Interior," with Lady in pink satin dress, playing on harpsichord (beautifully executed)
4	GUIDO....................	" The Virgin and Child," with St. Francis and St. C tharine kneeling—(on copper)
5	DIETRICHY...............	" The Fête Champêtre,"—a lovely garden scene
6	....	" Portrait of Louis XIII."—small whole length
7	SLINGELANDT............	" Interior," with Violin Player and other Figures
8	GUIDO....................	" The Grecian Daughter,"—very finely treated
9	GREUZE....................	" Girl Meditating," dressed with black scarf, hat, an feathers
10	MENESES...................	" The Apotheosis of a Saint," after Murillo
11	JAN STEEN...............	" Lady in Red Boddice at the Poultry Market"—a work of high quality
12	A. KAUFFMAN.............	" The Judgment of Paris"—exquisitely treated
13	ROBERT LEFEVRE.........	" The Sacrifice of Innocence,"—a masterly work of this admired Artist
14	....	" WHOLE LENGTH PORTRAIT OF THE EMPRESS CATHARINE OF RUSSIA," *executed in the highest style of Art, in a very splendid gilt frame, with presentation inscription in silver*
15	....	" The Adoration of the Virgin,"—(on panel)
16	....	" King of Prussia," or horseback

THIRD DAY'S SALE.

LOT		
17	SCHRŒDER	"Head of a Lady"—(in Crayons)
18		"Lord Chesterfield"—(in Crayons)
19		Small Drawing, "Heloise"
20	EVERDINGEN	"Mountain Scene in Norway"—very effective
21		"Sleeping Venus"—gilt frame
22		"View of Family Mansion
23		Ditto ditto
24		Ditto ditto
25		A pair of Prints, "The Baring Family," after Sir T. Lawrence
26		Three ditto—"T. Littledale, Esq.," and others
27		Sundries
28		Ditto
29		Ditto
30		Ditto

BRONZES, &c.

31 AN EXQUISITE ANTIQUE BRONZE APOLLO, *of the finest Grecian work, with inscription, Maris C. D. V. N. A. J. O. V. Oratus præ F. E. pius præ feciurs spaci - i uni. d. s. d.*

32 ANTINOUS, on marble plinth (one arm broken) a very fine antique work

33 APOLLO—an exquisite small figure, on giallo plinth

34 A Speculum, with three figures, in slight relief, and Etruscan inscription

35 A TALL CIRCULAR ETRUSCAN VESSEL AND COVER, with figures on top, on Lion's claw feet, rings at side, the surface engraved with figures of most elegant design, the lid engraved with Nereids

36 A Gladiator Reclining—a very fine work of art

37 A Dancing Figure on pedestal

38 A ditto, Roman Slave

39 A ditto, Venus

40 Pair of Swan Ornaments

41 Sundries

42 Ditto

43 Pair of Antique Snuffers

D

THIRD DAY'S SALE.

LOT

AMPHORA, &c.

44 A MAGNIFICENT AMPHORA OF NOLAN WARE—Tityus, at Delphos, carrying off Latona—Apollo and Diana on each side

The subject of this Vase is unique, bearing the names of the figures—on the other side an Agonoteta is prepared to instruct three Athletæ, whose names are inscribed, also the name of the owner of the Vase,—23½ inches high.

45 A ditto, with "Combat of Warriors," 16 inches high

46 A VERY FINE AMPHORA OF NOLAN WARE, with combat of five figures, and a warrior, herald, &c.—the figures heightened with purple and white, on red red ground—18 inches high

47 A BEAUTIFUL PANATHENAIC VASE, of Nolan ware, with figure of Minerva, &c., 21 inches high (*from the Durand Collection*)

48 A VERY CURIOUS LAMP, in the form of a lobster's claw, of Nolan ware, with a youth reposing, inscribed Καλος

49 A VERY FINE TWO-HANDLED CYLIX, with shepherds and sixteen figures dancing

50 A DITTO, Ulysses, &c.

51 A LARGER DITTO, with fauns, chariots, &c.

52 A DITTO, with a female holding a procos, and a warrior about to pour incense on an altar, inscribed Hoγλις Καλο

53 A RHYTON, in form of a stag's head with antlers, winged female seated on the lip

54 A VERY FINE DITTO, with head of the Indian Bacchus, heightened with white and frieze of leaves above

55 A SUPERB PELICE, WITH COVER, with Hercules in the lion's skin, and inscriptions in Greek

LIMOSINE ENAMELS, &c.

56 An oblong Plaque, with triumph of Cupids inscribed, "Maugre Fortune"

57 Ditto, Christ at the Feast, with Magdalen washing his feet—ebony frame

58 Ditto, Our Saviour and the Apostles,—ebony frame

59 Salt Cellar, with "Labours of Hercules, Female Bust," &c. Dated 1555

60 Ditto, "Laura," and female figures round the side in colours

61 A fine Tazza, with design—"Jacob's Dream," masks and arabesques beneath

62 A ditto, with Abraham and Melchizedek in brilliant colours, masks and arabesques outside

63 An oblong Plaque,—Æneas & Achates sacrificing oxen, partly pencilled with gold

64 A ditto,—Æneas and Creusa—Anchises and Ascanius (inscribed)

65 A ditto, "Bacchus," &c.

66 A ditto, Scriptural Subject

THIRD DAY'S SALE.

LOT

67 A LARGE TAZZA, with design—Moses and the Israelites fighting (a little injured)

68 A SUPERB OVAL SALVER, "Joseph before Pharoah," with border of arabesques, and fine arabesques beneath

69 A large Dish in Raffaelle ware

70 Three ditto—Fruit dishes

71 A pair of Stands

72 A rich blue Vase, with ormolu handle, stand, and spout

73 Another with crest

74 A set of three Vases, mounted in ormolu

75 A pair of fine high blue China Vases, with rich ormolu ornaments and stand

76 A blue China Jar with cover

77 A ditto with brass top

78 A small Marble Vase on pedestal

79 Sundries

80 Head of Jupiter

81 Fine Marble Bust (life size)

82 Ditto of Pope Leo, in his Pontifical vestments

83 A Roman Urn, with handles

84 A pair of ditto, Pateras

85 The Tomb of Scipio in marble

86 A white marble Tazza

87 A ditto with Sphinxes

88 A curious Watch Stand in marble

89 A pair of curious stained glass Flemish Pictures. Dated 1660

90 A gilt frame with 7 circular ditto

91 Two frames for miniatures

92 Model of a Church

93 A curious antique casket

94 A wood carving—pair of Japanese Sandals

95 A Medallion

96 A Squirrel Ornament in China

97 Curious China Tea Pot

98 A ditto— Cups and Saucers

99 Sundry Curiosities

100 Sundries

101 Ditto

End of Third Day's Sale.

D 2

FOURTH DAY'S SALE,

AT RUSHTON HALL, NEAR KETTERING, NORTHAMPTONSHI

ON THURSDAY, 9TH AUGUST, 1855,

Commencing at Eleven for Twelve o'Clock precisely.

No. 38, BACK BED ROOM.

LOT

389 A brass mounted fender, set of fire irons, and 3 pieces of Venetian carpet

390 Three sheep-skin mats, 2 chairs, and a wainscot dressing table and glass

391 A wainscot washstand, white fittings, towel horse, and small glass and dr table

392 A wainscot chest of five drawers

393 A 3 feet 6 iron tent bedstead, striped furniture

394 A palliasse and two horse hair bolsters

395 A wool mattress

396 A feather bed, bolster, and pillow

397 Pair of blankets and coverlid

398 A stump bedstead

399 A wool mattress, 2 blankets and coverlid

400 A feather bed, bolster and pillow

No. 39, RIGHT HAND FRONT BED ROOM.

401 A brass top fender and fire irons, and four pieces of carpet

402 Three chairs and covers

403 An easy chair covered with chintz

404 A deal painted press with sliding front and two drawers under

405 A ditto ditto

406 A japanned tray top dressing table with drawer

407 A swing dressing glass, a mahogany towel horse, and piece of Venetian car

408 A mahogany commode and two towel horses

FOURTH DAY'S SALE.

CORRIDOR.

LOT
409 Four mahogany chairs, seats stuffed, in red morocco, and Holland cover
410 An easy chair stuffed with horse hair
411 A rosewood cheffonier, with gallery top, on pillars, silk back
412 A wood basket and cover, and a gothic chair
413 Sundries

FIRST FLOOR.

No. 7, SOUTH FRONT BED CHAMBER.

414 A steel mounted fender with standards and set of fire irons
415 A japanned coal hod with cover and wire guard
416 The handsome Brussels carpet as planned to bed & dressing room, about 40 yds.
417 A Brussels hearth rug to match
418 A ditto
419 A ditto
420 Holland carpet covers to both rooms, about 40 yards
421 A handsome inlaid mahogany canopy French bedstead, with chintz pattern furniture, lined and fringed
422
423 The Holland covering over bedstead
424 A palliasse in ticken
425 A horsehair mattress
426 A wool bed
427 A ditto ditto, feather bolster, and one pillow
428 A cotton blanket and two woollen ditto
429 A Marseilles quilt and a cotton sheet
430 A MAHOGANY INLAID LADY'S WARDROBE, with shelf, shifting rod, and hooks, 5 feet 6 inches wide and 8 feet high
431 A mahogany pedestal library table with leather top and drawer
432 A carved mahogany frame easy chair, stuffed with horse hair, in chintz, and extra chintz cover
433 A FRENCH COUCH *en suite*, with inlaid mahogany frame, spring squab & bolster stuffed with hair, and one down pillow in chintz, and cover to ditto
434 A mahogany tray top pot cupboard and a ditto towel horse
435 Four Spanish mahogany carved chairs with hair seats in chintz *en suite*

FOURTH DAY'S SALE.

LOT

436 A mahogany pedestal writing table

437 A pair of chintz curtains to large bay window *en suite*, valens fringed, r(tassels, brass rods, &c.

438 Holland covering over ditto

439 A chimney glass in gilt frame, 60 inches by 48 inches

440 A bronze French clock under glass shade

No. 8, DRESSING ROOM.

441 A steel mounted fender, standards, and set of fire-irons

442 A japanned coal hod, brass wire guard, and boot-jack

443 A mahogany bidet and pan

444 A Queensware foot-bath and jug, and towel horse

445 A mahogany tray top dressing table, with two drawers, 3 feet 6

446 A box dressing glass, with drawer

447 A mahogany commode front chest of 5 drawers

448 Sundries

No. 9, FRONT SITTING ROOM, ADJOINING.

449 A steel mounted scroll fender with standards, set of fire irons, and brass g

450 The handsome Brussels carpet to room (about 17 yards)

451 A Brussels hearthrug to match

452 The Holland carpet covering

453 An elegant carved frame carriole Couch, spring seat and back, stuffe hair, in light blue silk damask, and cotton cover to ditto

454 Four ditto chairs *en suite*

455 A ditto elbow chair *en suite* and Holland cover

456 A pair of elegant silk damask Curtains to bay window *en suite*, line silk, silk fringe, ropes and tassels, gilt ornaments, rods, rings, &c.

457 A curiously inlaid marquetrie and ebony Cabinet, with 9 drawe: cupboard, on twisted pillar legs

458 A noble Chimney Glass in handsome gilt frame, plate 72 inches by 36

459 An elegant French Clock in ormolu under glass shade

FOURTH DAY'S SALE.

No. 14, HALL.

LOT

460 A handsome bronze and steel fender with brass ornaments and standards, 6 ft. 6 in. wide

461 A set of bronze and steel fire irons

462 A japanned sarcophagus coal receiver with brass handles and paw feet

463 A brass wire guard, 2 ft. 3 in. wide

464 A handsome rosewood frame barometer (by *Leret, Rouen*) and bracket

465 A ditto thermometer

466 A carved and polished oak card table, lined with drab cloth

467 A ditto square library table, 3 feet, and cover

468 A pair of ditto whatnots

469 A ditto loo table on pillar and claw, 4 feet, drab cloth top and cloth cover

470 A ditto ditto, 5 feet, and cloth cover

471 A HANDSOME DITTO OCTAGON HALL TABLE, 7 feet diameter, with massive carved pillar and holland cover

472 A HANDSOME SILK AND EMBROIDERED TAPESTRY TABLE COVER WITH SILK LINING, yards by

473 A circular seat *en suite*, in window, stuffed with horse hair in drab damask, five large back cushions, and four small ditto

474 A piece of Brussels carpet to window and recess, 6 yards

475 Eight carved and polished oak chairs, backs and seats stuffed with horse hair in rick damask, and Holland covers

476 Six Gothic carved ditto *en suite*, Holland covers

477 Six ditto ditto

478 Six ditto elbow ditto and covers

479 Six ditto ditto

480 A high back elbow easy chair *en suite* with cover

481 A ditto and cover

482 A ditto music chair with screw seat

483 A handsome carved rosewood framed sofa, stuffed with horse hair, squab and 2 bolsters and feather pillow, in crimson moreen, and Holland cover

484 A ditto ditto

485 A pair of drab damask curtains to bay window, trimmed with gimp and lined

486 A pair of ditto ditto, 12 breadths by $1\frac{3}{4}$ yards

487 A wood basket with cover

FOURTH DAY'S SALE.

LOT

488 A HANDSOME RICHLY CARVED OAK ANCIENT CABINET, WITH PILLAR FRON NUMEROUS DRAWERS, CUPBOARDS, AND ANTIQUE FITTINGS (date 1637), 8 fe 3 high, 7 feet wide

489 A GRAND PIANOFORTE, by *Clementi & Co.* (6½ octaves), in carved mahoga case, wainscot stand and brass castors, leather cover

490 A CAPITAL FULL SIZED MAHOGANY BILLIARD TABLE, HANDSOMELY CARVED PILL LEGS, lined with green cloth, by *Burroughes and Watts*, Holland cover

491 A mahogany marker, by *Thurston*, a circular mahogany cue stand, 11 cues a maces

492 A carved oak cue stand and 20 cues

493 A billiard lamp and iron crane

494 Two sheep skin rugs, 4 spittoons, and a mahogany letter box

495 An elegant japanned and gilt India screen with 8 folds

496 Four oak hall chairs

497 Four ditto

No. 16, DINING ROOM.

498 An elegant bronze polished steel fender with standards, 6 feet 6 wide

499 A set of handsome bronze and steel fire irons

500 A japanned coal receiver and cover

501 A ditto

502 A capital Brussels carpet to room, about 13 yards by 8

503 A ditto hearth rug to match

504 A large damask crumb cloth in drab and crimson, 10 yards by 3½

505 Four mahogany carved frame chairs with scroll legs, backs and seats stuffed v horse hair, in crimson morocco, and Holland covers

506 A carved mahogany frame high back Easy chair, stuffed with horse hai crimson Morocco leather

507 A ditto ditto

508 A ditto elbow ditto, with extending frame and shifting back, loose sq Holland cover

509 A mahogany frame 3-leaf cheval fire screen, in crimson damask, Holland c

510 A ditto ditto (smaller)

511 A ditto 1-leaf ditto, Holland cover

512 A 3-folding fire screen, mahogany frame, Holland cover

513 Four ditto chair back screens

514 An elliptic front inlaid mahogany sideboard with cellaret and plate drawers

FOURTH DAY'S SALE.

LOT

515 A mahogany pedestal sideboard with cellaret, plate drawers and cupboards, 7 feet wide

516 A RICHLY CARVED MAHOGANY PEDESTAL SIDEBOARD on paw feet and plinths, cellaret, plate drawers and cupboards, 8 feet wide, and holland cover

517 A ditto ditto and holland cover

518 A handsome mahogany Sarcophagus wine cellaret with richly carved paw feet, and holland cover

519 Ditto ditto, holland cover

520 A ditto ditto, plainer

521 A polished mahogany circular dumb waiter, rising frame, on pillar and claw

522 A ditto ditto

523 A ditto *wine table* with tray

524 A japanned plate warmer

525 A set of mahogany dining tables, 5 feet wide by 8 feet 10 in length, on pillar legs

526 A circular mahogany extending dining table, 6 feet 6 in. diameter

527 A BRONZE PILLAR with marble pedestal, eagle ornaments, and *ormolu* branches for 7 lights, also blue silk cover

528 A ditto ditto

529 A pair of ditto

530 A HANDSOME PARISIAN CLOCK, in marble and *ormolu*, with fine bronze figure ornaments (Delbevez)

531 A mahogany pot cupboard

532 Sundries

No. 36, LIBRARY.

533 A brass fender, set of fire irons, wire guard, and japanned coal receiver with cover

534 A pair of bronze candelabras with branches for four lights each

535 A HANDSOME PARISIAN CLOCK, in sienna marble, with bronze relief figure of *Achilles*

536 Eight rosewood carved frame chairs, seats stuffed with hair in crimson morocco, with holland covers

537 A ditto carved rosewood Sofa, *en suite*, squab stuffed with horse hair, and 2 pillows crimson morocco, and holland cover

538 A ditto pillar and claw Sofa table with four drawers, 4 feet 6

539 A ditto Loo table, *en suite*

540 A PAINTED MAHOGANY GOTHIC WINGED BOOK-CASE with folding glazed doors and cupboards under, 9 feet 6 wide, 10 feet 6 high

541 Ditto ditto to correspond 16 feet wide, 10 feet 6 high

542 A pair of folding steps

E

FOURTH DAY'S SALE.

PLATED.

LOT

543 A Pickle Stand with gadroon, silver edges, and 4 bottles

544 An elegant Cruet Stand, with silver edges, and 8 cut cruets, *silver tops*

545 An elegant Liqueur Frame, with richly chased silver edges, pair of decanter stands and cut decanters, and 12 drinking cups gilt inside

546 Three pair of high candlesticks and 2 pair of branches

547 Two pairs of richly chased ditto

548 Two pairs of ditto

549 Two pairs of ditto and a pair of 3-light branches

550 Three pair of high candlesticks

551 Three pair of ditto

552 A pair of chamber ditto with extinguishers

553 A pair of ditto ditto, snuffer tray and snuffers

554 A snuffer tray, 2 pairs of snuffers, 3 mounted corks and 2 labels

555 Six mounted corks and 2 strainers

556 A pair of large Meat Dishes, with gadroon silver edges

557 A pair of ditto

558 A pair of ditto (smaller)

559 Set of four Hash Dishes, Covers and Stands

560 A ditto ditto

561 A pair of hot dishes

562 A pair of ditto

563 A large Turbot Dish and Strainer

564 A ditto ditto

565 Sundries

566 Ditto

567 An oak plate chest, iron bound

End of Fourth Day's Sale.

FIFTH DAY'S SALE,

AT RUSHTON HALL, NEAR KETTERING, NORTHAMPTONSHIRE,

ON FRIDAY, THE 10TH OF AUGUST, 1855,

Commencing at Eleven for Twelve o'Clock precisely.

LIBRARY OF BOOKS.

FOLIO.

LOT.		VOLS.
1	General Atlas, by D'Anville and Robert (62 *copper-plates*)	
2	Origin of Commerce, *half bound*	2
3	Novum Testamentum, Cantab, 1642	
4	Imagination, par Delille (*plates*), Paris, 1806	2
5	Heloise and Abelard, *boards* (*plates*), Paris, 1796	3
6	Les Saisons, par St. Lambert, Paris, 1796	1
7	L'homme des Champs, par Delille, Strasbourg, *calf gilt*, 1802	
8	Wilkinson's General Atlas	
9	Cary's English Atlas and Voyages dě Siberie	1
10	Encyclopædie ou Dictionnaire des Sciences, par M. Diderot, Paris	33
11	Baker's History and Antiquities of the County of Northampton (5 *parts*)	
12	JOURNAL DES DEBATS, 1827 to 1851, *half bound in calf*	29
13	GAZETTE DES TRIBUNEAUX, 1826 to 1831, *calf*	3
14	Sundries	
15	Ditto	

QUARTO.

16	Histoire Universelle *calf*, Amsterdam, 1776	44
17	British Atlas, 1810; Gray's Poems (Parma, printed by Bodoni, 1793); and Keppel's Personal Narrative, 1827	
18	Weld's Travels through North America; Ive's Voyage, 1773; and Buckingham's Travels in Mesopotamia, 1827	
19	Beechey's Northern Coast of Africa, 1828; Campbell's Journey to India, 1796; Burckhardt's Travels in Arabia, and Campaignes des Prussiens, 1787	

E 2

FIFTH DAY'S SALE.

LOT		VOLS.
20	Art of Painting, by Reynolds, 1783, and Hogarth's Analysis of Beauty, 1753	
21	Existence de Dieu (*plates*) Amsterdam, 1727, and Ruses Innocentes, Paris, 1688	
22	Noble's College of Arms, 1805, and Burke's Works	4
23	History of Great Britain, by Hollingbery, 2 vols., 1787; and Royal Tribes of Wales, by Yorke, 1799	
24	Park's Travels in Africa (*plates*) 1799, and Clarke's Travels in Russia	2
25	Ovid's Metamorphoses, in Latin and French, 1761 (*plates*) *morocco gilt*	4
26	Planter's Helvetic Confederacy, 1800, 2; and Memoirs of the Prince of Orange, 1	3
27	Monarchie Prussienne, 1788	4
28	Transactions of the Horticultural Society (7 *parts*)	
29	Dr. Styles's Holy Bible, 2; and Hosea, by Bishop Horsley, 1	3
30	Boyer's French Dictionary	
31	Marin's French and Dutch Dictionary, 1; ditto, Dutch and French, 1, 1782.	2
32	Marin's Dutch and French Dictionary, 1; ditto French and Dutch, 1793	2
33	Ludwig's German Dictionary; ditto English and German; Boyer's French and English, and English and French Dictionary, *bound* 2	
34	English and Dutch Dictionary, by Sewell; Plinii Opera, 1751..............................	
35	Fifteen Maps, various (*some in cases*)	
36	Sundries	
37	Ditto	

OCTAVO.

LOT		VOLS.
38	Warton's Virgil (*plates*), Dodsley, 1753, 4; Blarke's Homer, 2..............................	6
39	The Metropolitan Magazine..............................	13
40	The Revolution in Sweden, by Sheridan, 1 vol., and 13 vols. various	14
41	Histoire du Bas-Empire, by Lebeau, 1780, *half calf*	27
42	Spectacle de la Nature 1743 (*plates*) *half calf*	8
43	Rollin, Histoire Romaine, 1771, *half calf*	16
44	ŒUVRES COMPLETES DE VOLTAIRE, 1826, *calf*	70
45	Œuvres complètes de Marmontel, 1818, *calf*	18
46	Œuvres complètes de Regnard, 1820, *calf*	6
47	Œuvres de Andrieux, 1823 (*plates*), *calf*	4
48	Œuvres de Montesquieu, 1827, *calf*	8
49	Poésies de Chatelieu, 1825, *calf*	1
50	Extracts in Prose, 2; and ditto in Verse, 1791, 2	4

FIFTH DAY'S SALE.

LOT		VOLS.
51	Bolingbroke's Letters on History, 1752, 2; Gilpin's History of England, 1798, (*plates*); Letters from the East, 1826; and Harrison's Life of Nelson, 1806, *russia*, 2........	
52	Roscoe's Memoires of Scipio de Ricci, 1829, *calf*........	2
53	Sundries	
54	ENCYCLOPÆDIE MODERNE, PAR M COURTIN, (*plates*)	26
55	The British Library........	2
56	ŒUVRES DE BUFFON, *half calf*........	26
57	Cours de Literature........	16
58	Delille's Works, (*plates*)	14
59	Les Pensées de Pascal, 1826, *green calf gilt*, 2; Discours sur L'Histoire par Bonnet, 1825, *calf gilt*, 2........	4
60	Oraisons Funèbres, par Bonnet, 1825, *calf gilt*, 1; ditto, de Flècher, 1825; Sermons de Boullier, 2........	4
61	Essais de Montaigne, *calf gilt*........	5
62	Œuvres, completes, de Legouve (*fine plates*)	3
63	Corneille's Works........	4
64	Tristan, par Marchangy	6
65	Histoire d'Alexander I. of Russia, 2; Œuvres d'Hamilton, 2; Histoire de Clergi, 1; and Œuvres de Bertin, 1........	6
66	Lettres à Emilie, par Demoustier, (*plates*) *green calf*, 2; and La Moquer Amoureux, par Gay, 2........	4
67	Mémoires du Duc St. Simon, 1826	6
68	Paley's Evidences........	2
69	Œuvres de Le Sage	12
70	Œuvres complètes de Crebillon, *blue calf*, 1824, 2; Théâtre de Delavigne (*plates*) *calf*, 2	4
71	Œuvres Choisies de J. B. Rousseau, 1; Œuvres de Rochefoucault, *half-bound*; ditto de Clement Marot; ditto de Malfilatre, *calf gilt*; ditto de Gresset, 1; ditto de Jerome, 1	
72	Le Renégat, 2; Revolution du 10 Aout, 2........	4
73	Histoire du Bible, *curious woodcuts*, 1802; and Paley's Evidences 2........	
74	Les Martyrs, par Chateaubriand, 2; Mythologie comparée avec L'Histoire 2; and Voyage sur le Rhin (*fine plates*)	
75	Œuvres de Picard, 10; and Voyage en Italie, 7	17
76	Œuvres de Millevoye	4
77	Mémoires d'une Femme de Qualité, 4; and Romans de Voltaire 3	7
78	Bonnet's Nature, 3; and Poesies de Malherbe, 1, *calf gilt*........	4

FIFTH DAY'S SALE.

LOT		VOLS.
79	Heptameron Français (*plates*) *green calf*	3
80	Voyage de La Perouse	4
81	La Philosophie de la Nature (*plates*), 3; and Mémoire par Montlosier, 1	4
82	Mémoires d'une Contemporaine, 1828, *half-bound*	8
83	Decameron de Boccace 1757, (*plates*), *calf gilt*	5
84	Chronicles du Temps de Charles IX. 1829, 1; Œuvres de Condillac, 1; and Œuvres de St. Bernard, 1	3
85	Mémoires de Duc de Lauzun, 2; Dissertation sur la Caffée, 1757; and Cinq Mars, par de Vigney, Paris, 1827, 2	
86	Mémoires des Contemporaries, 1824	4
87	Œuvres de Rabelais, 1824 (*plates*), *calf*	9
88	Œuvres de Destouche, 1820 (*plates*)	6
89	Voyage du Jeune Anacharsis en Grèce; par Barthelemy, *calf*	7
90	Œuvres complètes de La Fontaine, 1826, *calf*	6
91	Œuvres de J. J. Rousseau, 1827, *calf*	20
92	Mémoires du Cardinal Retz, 1820	6
93	Capefige, Histoire de Philippe Auguste, 1829	4
94	Mémoires de Sully, 1822	6
95	Manuel d'Estampes	3
96	Œuvres de Bonfflers, 2; Mémoires de Madame Haussett, 1; and Reproduction de l'Homme, par Touchant, *calf*, 1	4
97	Voyages dans L'Isle de France, par Brunet, 1; Voyages en Afrique, par Vaillant, (*plates*); and Histoire de la Columbie, 1826	4
98	Barruet's Jacobinism, abrégè, 5; and Manuelle la Banque, 1	6
99	Siecles de la Poésie Française, Amsterdam, 1808, 1; Anecdotes de Russie, 1797; Mercier Neologie, 1801, 2; Domerque Manuel des Français, 1805, 1	4
100	Tragédies et Drames, par Ducis, 1815; Comedies, Paris, 1760; Petrarque et Laure, by Genlis, 1819	
101	Mémoires Ferdinand VII; Cours de Mathematique; Constitution de l'Angletèrre; and Campagnes du Suworow	
102	Mémoires de Mdlle. Montpensier, 1776, *calf*	8
103	Leçons Latines, 1818, *calf*	2
104	QUARTERLY REVIEW, from 1809 to 1834	50
105	BUFFON'S NATURAL HISTORY, 1812	20
106	Gregory's Economy of Nature, 3; Lounder's Common place Book, 2; and Robertson's History of Charles V., 4	9
107	Smith's Wealth of Nations, 3; Johnson's Lives of the English Poets, 4	7
108	Rippon's History of England	21

FIFTH DAY'S SALE.

LOT		VOLS.
109	Whiston's Josephus, 1811	4
110	Kerr's Voyages and Travels, 1824, *calf*	18
111	Playfair's French Revolution, 1795, 1; Russell's Modern Europe, 1814, 6	7
112	Chesterfield's Miscellanies	4
113	Lavater's Physiognomy	4
114	Paley's Natural Theology, 1802, 1; Lancelot's Tour to La Grand Chartreuse, 1813, 1; History of Bees, 1; and Natural History, 1791, 3	6
115	Goldsmith's History of England, 1809, 4; ditto History of Rome, 2; and ditto History of Greece, 2	8
116	Ferguson's Roman History, 1791	6
117	Tales of an Antiquary, 1828, 3; and Zillah, 4	7
118	Tales of the O'Hara Family, 3; The Trials of Life, 3; and Tales of a Voyager, 3	9
119	The Night Watch, 2; Truckleborough Hall, 3; Tales of the West, 2; and Stanton Hall, *calf*, 3	10
120	La Fontaine's Fables, (*plates*) 1806; Coleman's Terence, 1; Paley's Evidences, 2; and Chalmers' Estimate, 2	6
121	Ketts' Elements, 1803, 2; and the Guardian, 1822, *calf*, 2	4
122	Pope's Works, *calf*	9
123	Elegant Extracts, in prose and verse, 1809	3
124	Sundries	
125	History of the French Consulate, by Barré, 1804, 1; Wraxall's House of Valois, 1807, 2; and Williams's Digest of the Statute Law, 1809, 2	5
126	Goldsmith's History of England, 1812, 4; ditto History of Rome, 2; ditto History of Greece, 2	8
127	Hoole's Orlando Furioso, 1785	5
128	Warton's History of English Poetry, 1824, *calf*	4
129	Hume and Smollett's History of England, 1791, *roan*	13
130	Robertson's Charles V., 4; and Watson's Philip II., 3	7
131	Adam Smith's Nature and Causes, 1801, 4; Delolme on the Constitution, 1; and Bank of England, 1	6
132	Pliny's Letters, 1757, 2; Thompson's Works, 1744, 3; Crispigni's Advice to her Son, 1813, 1; and Home's Elements of Criticism, 2	8
133	Elliott's Life of Wellington, 1815, *morocco*, 1; and Ireland's Hogarth, 3	4
134	Classical Tour through Italy, by Eustace, *calf*, 4; and The Indies in 1825, 1	5
135	Goldsmith's Works, 1792	7
136	Watts's Logic, 1768, 2; Edwards's Canons of Criticism, 1; Tour in Wales, 1; Ranel's Astronomy, 1; and Life of Blucher, 1	6

FIFTH DAY'S SALE.

LOT		VOLS.
137	United Service Journal from 1834 to 1838, *half calf*	15
138	Quarterly Review from 1834 to 1848 inclusive	10
139	Mémoires de Casanova, par lui-même, 1833, *unbound*	10
140	Guthrie's Geographical Grammar; Greek Lexicon, 1; Lempriere's Classical Dictionary; and Bibliotheque Portative, 3	6
141	Pilkington's Dictionary of Painters	2
142	Dictionnaire Française et Italien, 2; Price on Annuities, 2; Lempriere's Classical Dictionary; and French Dictionary, 1	6
143	Sundries	
144	Ditto	
145	Holtrop's English & Dutch Dictionary, and ditto Dutch & English	2
146	Walton's Angler (Major), 1824, *morocco gilt*, 1; and Elegant Epistles, 1	2
147	Roscoe's German Novelist, 4; and Kraft's Odes, *green morocco gilt*, 1	5
148	Vilcoke Dictionary, English & Dutch, and Bekman's History of Inventions	5
149	Brisson, Dictionaire de Physique, 6, and quarto vol. of plates	7
150	Dictionaire de Giovinettes, 1815, 2; Physiologie du Gôut, 2; Veneroni Grammaire, French & Italian; Essai de Perpectif, (*plates*) 2	6
151	Biographie Modern, Breslau, 1806, 4; Abrègé Historie de la Hollande, 4	8
152	Abrègé Chronicle de France; Grammaire Française, 1; English & Dutch Testament; L'Art d'Ecrire, 1	4
153	Kraft's Works, 3; Moore's Works, (imperfect) 4; Husband Hunting, vols. 2 and 3; Rebelles sur Charles V., 1852, *unbound*, 3; Souvenir de la Marquise, *unbound*, 3	15
154	Blackwood's Magazine & 11 others; Vaderlandsche Historie, Jan Wagenaar, 1792, 1; and Bowdler's Letters from Holland, 1	15
155	Sundries	

TWELVEMO.

LOT		VOLS.
156	BELL'S EDITION OF THE POETS OF GREAT BRITAIN, COMPLETE, FROM CHAUCER TO CHURCHILL, London, 1778, *calf*	101
157	Voyages of Christopher Columbus, 1828, *calf*	4
158	Bowdler's Poems, 1787, 2; The Prairie, 1827, *calf*, 3; and Cyril Thornton, 1827, 3	8
159	Shakespeare	8
160	SIR WALTER SCOTT'S NOVELS AND TALES, *calf*	42
161	Washington Irving's Works, *calf*	12
162	Sir Walter Scott's Poetical Works	8

FIFTH DAY'S SALE.

LOT.		VOLS.
163	Memoirs of Sheridan, by Moore, *morocco*, 2; and Lady Morgan's Works, 3...	5
164	Byron's Works, *blue calf*..........	5
165	Cowper's Poems, 2; Sketches of Persia, 2; and Ada Reis, 2	6
166	Shakespeare, by Reed	12
167	Capell's Shakespeare	10
168	Johnson's Lives of the Poets, 7; Blair's Rhetoric, 1	8
169	Tor Hill, 3; Hajji Baba, 2; and Coming Out, 3..........	8
170	Memoirs of Margravine of Anspach, 2; Tales of a Voyager, L'Exalté, 4; and Economy of Human Life, 1..........	7
171	Les Enfans, de deuxlits, par A. La Fontaine, Paris, 1822, *half-bound*, 4; L'Etudes de la Nature, par St. Pierre, 1788, 5..........	9
172	Precis, de L'Historie Universelle, par Anquetin..........	9
173	Siècle Louis XIV., 2; Lettres de Chesterfield, 4	6
174	D'Islande, Paris, 1823, 3; Le Coup de Badenoch, par Macaulay, 1828, 5......	8
175	L'Ecole de Mœurs, par Blanchard, Lyon, 1804	6
176	Plutarch's Lives, in French, 1724..........	8
177	La Découverte d'Auverigne, 1784..........	8
178	Lettres du Pope Clement XIV., 1776, 4; and Œuvres de Genlis, 1784, 7...	11
179	Considerations sur les Œuvres de Dieu, par Sturm, 1785, 3; and Les Traits de l'Histoire Sacrée et Poétique, 6..........	9
180	Histoire de Charles XII., par Voltaire, 1810, 1; La Logique, 1775, ; Zaydé, ; John Moore, par Bouchét, 2; Les Missionaires, par Rougemont, 1820, ; and Les Parvenus, 3	
181	Agathe, par V. Ducange, Paris, 1819, 2; Il Cadmo di Bagnoli, Pisa, 1821, *calf*, 2; Œuvres d'Horace, 1816, 2; Goldin Comedie Bellezzé della Italien, 1821, ; and Anquetil, Louis XIV., Paris, 1787, 4..........	
182	Fragments de Lettres Originels, 2; Poésies de Mad. Dufresnoy, ; and Mon Voisin Raymond, par Paul de Kock, Paris, 1826, 4..........	
183	ŒUVRES DE PIGNAULT LE BRUN, Paris, 1819..........	60
184	L'Homme du Monde, par M. Ancelot, Paris, 1827, 4; and Œuvres de Moliere, par M. de Voltaire, Leipzic, 1765, 5..........	9
185	Virgil, 1811, 3; Histoire de Guillaume III., 1703, 2; L'Esprit de la Ligne, 1770, 2; and Les Jeunes Femmes, 2..........	9
186	Contes à ma Fille, Bouilly, London, 1815, ; Conseilles à ma Fille, Bouilly, 1817, ; La Confession, Paris, 1830, 2; and Œuvres de La Fosse, 1755...	
187	Philosophie Morale, 1756, ; Chansons, 1825, 3; Amours et Aventures du Viscomte de Barras, 1816, 3; Vingt-quatre Heures d'une Femme Sensible, 1825, ; and 7 various	

F

FIFTH DAY'S SALE.

LOT		VOLS.
188	Œuvres de Florian, 9; Gil Blas, 4; and Mémoires d'un Homme de Qualité, 1808, 4	17
189	Bibliotheque Portative, par Levizac, 1803, 3; Œuvres de Desperaux, 5	8
190	Italy, by Lady Morgan, Paris, 1821, *calf*, 5; The Devil on Two Sticks, 6;	11
190*	The Red Rover, *calf*, 3; and Spectator, 8	11
191	Dryden's Virgil, 1806, 4; Shenstone, 1; Rasselas, 1; Sterne, 1; Francis's Horace, 1807, 4; and Plays, 8	19
192	Trimmer's Sacred History, 6; Goldsmith's Roman History, 1814; Zeluco, by Moore, 1803, 2; Gisborne's Poems, 1; ditto Works, 1; Rogers's Pleasures of Memory; Anne Matildà; and 8 various	21
193	Œuvres de Parry, 5; Histoirè de Russie, 2; St. Flour de Justini, 2; Directoire, 1; L'Ideé Fixè, 1830, 2; Journal of a Naturalist, 1; and 6 various	19
194	English Atlas, 1; Burder's Oriental Customs; Moral Essays; Missions, 2; Night Thoughts, 1; and 10 various	16
195	Dictionaire Histoire Naturel; Paris, 1768, 6; Dictionaire des Plantes de la France, 3; and Dictionaire French and Italien	10
196	Latin and Dutch Books, 6; Demonology, 1; and 16 others	23

End of Fifth Day's Sale, and First Portion of the Catalogue.

Inside the green house at the hall with John Cruikshank, Head Gardener on the right.

John Cruikshank, Head Gardener, with friend and his horse called Ajax.

CATALOGUE OF

THE VALUABLE EFFECTS

AT

RUSHTON HALL

NORTHAMPTONSHIRE.

RUSHTON HALL, NORTHAMPTONSHIRE.

A Catalogue

OF

THE CONTENTS OF

THE NOBLE MANSION

OF THE LATE

W. WILLIAMS HOPE, ESQ.,

RUSHTON HALL, NORTHAMPTONSHIRE,

Four Miles from Kettering, Twelve from Wellingborough, and Sixteen from Northampton,

COMPRISING THE

ELEGANT PARISIAN FURNITURE,

CNINA, GLASS, &c.,

Wardrobes of Bed and Table Linen,

CELLAR OF CHOICE WINES,

FRENCH COOKERY AND UTENSILS,

FOWLING PIECES,

LIVE AND DEAD FARMING STOCK;

WHICH WILL BE SOLD BY AUCTION BY

MR. C. WARTON,

ON THE PREMISES,

ON MONDAY, THE 13TH OF AUGUST, 1855,

AND FOUR FOLLOWING DAYS, AT ELEVEN FOR TWELVE O'CLOCK EACH DAY.

May be Viewed on Friday and Saturday previous to the Sale, and Catalogues had (1*s.* each) at Hope's Arms, Rushton; Royal Hotel, Kettering; the Angel, Market Harborough; the Royal Hotel, Rugby; the Bell, Leicester; Angel, Peterborough; George Hotel, Northampton; the Hind, Wellingborough; Swan, Bedford; of **Messrs. ROWLAND and HACON, Solicitors, No. 31, Fenchurch Street;** and of

Mr. C. WARTON, Auctioneer and Estate Agent, No. 7, Union Court, Old Broad Street, Removed from Threadneedle Street.

ORDER OF SALE.

RUSHTON HALL, NEAR KETTERING, NORTHAMPTONSHIRE.

SIXTH DAY'S SALE, Monday, 13th August.

THE FURNITURE OF SEVERAL PRINCIPAL AND SECONDARY BED ROOMS—PICTURE FRAMES—AND PORTION OF THE LINEN.

SEVENTH DAY'S SALE, Tuesday, 14th August.

THE FURNITURE OF THE PRINCIPAL AND TWO OTHER BED ROOMS AND THE DRAWING ROOM—ALSO THE LIBRARY OF MUSICAL WORKS.

EIGHTH DAY'S SALE, Wednesday, 15th August.

THE CELLAR OF CHOICE WINES—THE FOWLING PIECES, GUNS, AND SWORDS—GARDEN PLANTS—SWANS, BOATS, &c.

NINTH DAY'S SALE, Thursday, 16th August.

THE FURNITURE OF LINEN ROOM—SEVERAL BED ROOMS—HALL—PORTION OF THE LINEN—SERVICES OF CUT GLASS AND CHINA—AND FRENCH COOKERY UTENSILS.

TENTH DAY'S SALE, Friday, 17th August.

THE FURNITURE IN BAILIFF'S HOUSE IN THE PARK—THE BROOD MARES AND COLTS—THE LIVE AND DEAD FARMING STOCK—AND THE MATERIALS, &c., IN OUT-BUILDINGS.

NOTE—The Sale will commence at Eleven for Twelve o'Clock punctually each day and Lots will be delivered between the hours of Nine and Eleven on the day.

NOTE.—Trains leave the Euston Square Station for Northampton and Wellingborough, from which places conveyances may be obtained.

CONDITIONS OF SALE.

1. *The highest bidder to be the buyer, and if any dispute arise between two or more bidders, the lot in dispute shall be immediately put up again and re-sold.*

2. *No person to advance less than One Shilling at each bidding; Five Shillings above five pounds; and so on in proportion.*

3. *The purchasers are, if required, positively to pay down a deposit of Five Shillings in the Pound on each lot, and give in their names and places of abode, in default of which the lot shall be put up again and re-sold, and such defaulter's bidding will not be taken again.*

4. *The remainder of the purchase-money to be paid and the lots taken away, with all faults, at the buyer's expense before the* 23rd *of August,* 1855, *and in default of this the auctioneer will not be responsible for loss or damage to any lots remaining, the sole risk being with the purchaser, who shall pay for a man's time attending to deliver (over and above the time allowed), at* 5s. *per day, or the lots may be forfeited at the option of the auctioneer.*

5. *Any allowance claimed for deficiences to be calculated by the auctioneer, in proportion to the purchase-money given, and in no case to be subject to other estimates or after sales, and no allowance will be made at all for errors of description, or for presumed deficiences, after the lots are once delivered to the purchaser.*

Lastly,—Upon failure of complying with the above conditions, the money deposited in part payment shall be forfeited, the lot or lots remaining uncleared after the time specified, shall be re-sold by public or private sale, and the deficiency (if any) by such second sale, together with all charges attending the same, shall be made good by the defaulter or defaulters at this present sale.

SIXTH DAY'S SALE,

AT RUSHTON HALL, NEAR KETTERING, NORTHAMPTONSHIRE,

ON MONDAY, 13TH AUGUST, 1855,

Commencing at Eleven for Twelve o'Clock precisely.

No. 40, BED ROOM.

LOT
571 Five pieces of carpetting, tin watercan, and a japanned corner washstand with fittings
572 A square ditto japanned washstand, and mahogany frame swing glass
573 A wainscot chest of five drawers
574 A ditto
575 Three chairs and a mahogany frame swing dressing glass
576 A mahogany ditto
577 An iron bedstead, with printed furniture
578 Ditto ditto
579 Ditto ditto
580 A palliasse
581 Ditto
582 Ditto
583 A hair mattress
584 A feather bed, bolster and pillow
585 Ditto ditto
586 Ditto ditto
587 A wool mattress
588 Ditto
589 Four blankets and a coverlet
590 Four ditto and a ditto
591 Five ditto and a ditto
592 Three pair of sheets

No. 25, LUMBER ROOM.

593 A wool bed and tick
594 Three bags of horse hair, about ½ cwt.
595 An iron bedstead

G

SIXTH DAY'S SALE.

LOT
596 Two copper coal scuttle scoops
597 A hall lamp
598 A rosewood Canterbury
599 Two mahogany tray stands, 6 extra drawers, 4 chairs various, and 2 chair cushions
600 An India japanned cabinet, with ten drawers
601 A field bedstead
602 Two marble slabs, foot warmer, and two slabs
603 A mahogany bidet and pan
604 A japanned washstand and fittings
605 A mahogany towel horse
606 A Queen's ware foot bath and jug
607

No. 5, FIRST FLOOR—EAST BED CHAMBER.

608 A steel mounted fender, with standards, and set of fire irons
609 A japanned coal hod with cover
610 A new Brussels hearth rug
611 A ditto ditto
612 An elegant Brussels carpet, planned to bed and dressing room, about 34 yards
613 Two Holland covers to ditto
614 A Handsome Spanish Mahogany French Bedstead, brass ornaments, with canopy top, and rich crimson damask hangings, fringed
615 A pair of window curtains *en suite*, with fringed valens, brass rods, rings, &c.
616 A palliasse
617 A capital horsehair mattress
618 A goose feather bed, bolster, and pillow
619 A wool bed in white cotton
620 Two blankets, a Marseilles quilt, and one sheet
621 An easy chair, stuffed with hair in scarlet morine, rosewood inlaid frame
622 A ditto leg rest, and wire fire guard
623 The Holland covering over bedstead
624 A chimney glass in gilt frame, plate 72 inches by 28 wide
625 A bronze French clock with glass shade
626 A handsome mahogany frame sofa, stuffed with hair in crimson damask, 2 down pillows, and Holland Cover
627 A mahogany tray top pot cupboard
628 A mahogany pedestal library table, with drawer and leather top
629

SIXTH DAY'S SALE.

No. 6, DRESSING ROOM.

LOT

630 A steel mounted fender, with standards, and set of fire irons
631 A japanned coal hod, with cover, and wire fire-guard
632 A new Brussels hearth rug
633 A chimney glass in gilt frame, plate 40 by 30 inches
634 A GENTLEMAN'S INLAID MAHOGANY WARDROBE, with plate glass panels, 48 inches by 28 inches, three shelves and drawer under
635 A Spanish mahogany chest of three drawers
636 A MAHOGANY INLAID WASHSTAND, with six drawers and cupboard, marble top and white and gold fittings
637 A mahogany tray top dressing table on turned legs, with two drawers
638 A swing dressing glass, with two drawers
639 A pair of crimson damask window curtains, fringed valens, brass rods, rings, &c.
640 A mahogany towel horse, a queen's ware foot bath, and water jug
641 An inlaid mahogany high-back chair, stuffed with hair in scarlet damask
642 A ditto Bergiere chair
643 The Brussels carpet on landing, about 16 yards
644 A wood basket with cover
645 A Holland damask cover to landing
646 A mahogany chair, stuffed in scarlet leather, and Holland cover
647 Sundries
648

No. 46, CHINA ROOM.

649 A slab iron fender, set of fire irons and deal painted table
650 A stout deal Pastry Counter with cupboards and tartlet drawers, 6 feet
651 A mahogany Pembroke table with drawers
652 Two mahogany butler's trays with stands, and deal stool
653 Three mahogany butler's trays, a mahogany slab and a door mat
654 Two japanned tea boards, 6 trays and 2 bread baskets
655 Two tea boards, 4 trays, 2 bread baskets and a knife tray
656 Six Moderator Lamps
657 Six ditto
658

G 2

SIXTH DAY'S SALE.

No. 47, LAUNDRY.

LOT

659 Stout framed deal top table, 4 feet wide 7 feet long
660 An oak ditto with 3 drawers
661 Four wood bottom chairs, a framed knife board and 2 brooms
662 An ironing board
663 Sundries

LINEN.

664 Two pairs of fine linen sheets
665 Two pairs ditto
666 Two pairs ditto
667 Three pairs ditto
668 Three pairs ditto
669 A white knotted counterpane and drab table cover
670 Set of drab damask window curtains
671 A pair of chintz window curtains lined with blue, and bed furniture to match
672 Two large damask table cloths
673 Two ditto
674 Three smaller ditto
675 Three ditto
676 Three ditto
677 Three ditto
678 Two dozen new table napkins
679 Two dozen ditto
680 Two dozen ditto
681 Two dozen huckaback towels
682 Three dozen ditto
683 Thirty-two pairs of footman's gloves
684 Twelve linen bath shirts
685 Three dozen knife cloths
686 Twenty-four jack towels
687 Two dozen cook's linen aprons
688 Two dozen ditto
690

SIXTH DAY'S SALE.

No. 49, IRONING ROOM.

LOT

691 A steel mounted fender, set of fire irons, guard, piece of oil cloth and coal hod

692 A stout deal framed ironing table, 8 feet by 6 feet

693 A square ditto, 5 feet by 4 feet

694 Two deal forms, 2 clothes horses and two coat ditto

695 Four rosewood japanned chairs with caned seats and cushions

696 Twelve clothes baskets

697 Twelve ditto and 2 coal scuttles

698

DAIRY.

699 A patent American churn

700 A stout deal board, 12 feet, on 3 tressels

701 A butter box, 2 cream trays, 2 tressels and 2 iron bars

702

GAME LARDER.

703 A framed deal table, 8 feet by 3 feet 6

704 A weighing machine with 4 weights

705 Two fly wire meat covers, 2 baskets, 2 pickling pans and chopper

706

CUPBOARDS, &c., IN PASSAGE.

707 A deal box, 7 brushes, brooms, &c., 2 coal scuttles, water can, and door mat

708 A wainscot linen press

709 A deal table with two drawers

710 A tin kettle and stand, tea tray, deal stand, boot jack, and 2 pieces of oilcloth

711

SCULLERY.

712 A slab iron fender and mahogany butler's tray,

713 A glass tub, 2 beer cans, 1 sieve, 1 chair, and 3 dish covers

714 Two copper tea kettles, and 5 ditto saucepans and lids

715 Two braziers, 4 iron saucepans, and 1 kettle

716 One large iron boiler, 2 frying pans, sundry small tins, and about 40 pieces of crockery

717

No. 50, SERVANTS' HALL.

LOT

718 A slab iron fender, a set of fire irons, and 2 hearth rugs
719 A wainscot round table
720 Twelve railed back Windsor chairs
721 A stout deal framed table, 12 feet long and 4 feet wide
722 A circular painted meat screen, lined with tin (opens at back)
723 Two forms, 4 dish covers, and 2 japanned coal scuttles
724 An eight day kitchen clock (by *Bates*, of *Kettering*)
725 Four tea trays, waiter, 5 brass candlesticks, bronze inkstand, knife box with kitchen knives and forks
726 A deal two-flap table and a copper warming pan
727 Five tin candlesticks, knife board, pail, candle box, chair, and coal scuttle
728 Five Moderator Lamps
729 Six ditto, various
730 Two ditto ditto
731 Twelve branch ditto
732 Twelve ditto

DAIRY, &c.

733 A 2 inch deal board (15 feet) on 3 tressels
734 A stout framed table, 6 feet
735 Six tin milk pans, a cream tin, milk tub, and 10 brown ware ditto
736 A dolly churn and 2 pails
737 A weighing machine and weights
738 A barrel churn
739 A bacon rack
740 Two iron scrapers, 2 washing tubs, and pail

MAN'S ROOM (IN LOFT).

741 An iron bedstead, fender, and guard
742 A japanned chest of four drawers
743 Thirteen chairs, various

SIXTH DAY'S SALE.

LOT
744 A mahogany pot cupboard and wainscot dressing table
745 Ditto loo table on pillar and claw
746 A stout stand, a fender, fire irons, and glass
747 A mahogany French bedstead
748 A rosewood cabinet with numerous drawers
749 Three chairs, towel horse, and wainscot commode

PICTURE FRAMES.

750 Four gilt picture frames, variou ssizes
751 Four ditto
752 Four ditto
753 Four ditto
754 Six ditto
755 Six ditto
756 Nine ditto
757 Three gallery ditto
758 Three ditto
759 Three ditto
760 Three ditto
761 Five ditto
762 Five ditto
763 Five ditto
764 Four very large ditto
765 Sundry frames, various
766 A quantity of gilt and metal cornice
767 Sundries
768 Ditto
769

End of Sixth Day's Sale.

SEVENTH DAY'S SALE,

AT RUSHTON HALL, NEAR KETTERING, NORTHAMPTONSHIRE,

ON TUESDAY, 14TH AUGUST, 1855,

Commencing at Eleven for Twelve precisely.

No. 1, SOUTH FRONT EAST BACK BED ROOM.

LOT

770 A brass mounted fender, fire irons, and guard
771 A Kidderminster carpet (16 yards)
772 A hearth rug
773 A 4 feet japanned French bedstead
774 Two wool mattresses
775 A feather bolster, 1 pillow, 4 blankets, and 2 counterpanes
776 Ditto washstand and fittings, glass, and 2 japanned chairs
777 A japanned frame dressing glass and towel horse

No. 2, FRONT EAST BED ROOM.

778 A Kidderminster carpet (12 yards)
779 A 3 ft. 6 in. japanned French bedstead
780 A horsehair mattress in ticking
781 A wool ditto, feather bolster and pillow
782 Four blankets and coverlid
783 A japanned washstand and fittings
784 A ditto dressing table with drawer and ditto swing glass
785 A ditto towel horse and 4 cane seat chairs
786 A wainscot chest of 5 drawers

No. 17, PRINCIPAL BED ROOM.

787 An ormolu and polished steel fender with standards
788 A set of fire irons and wire guard
789 A Brussels carpet to room (about 10 yards by 5½)

SEVENTH DAY'S SALE.

LOT

790 A Brussels hearth rug

791 A japanned coal receiver and cover

792 A HANDSOME INLAID SPANISH MAHOGANY FRENCH BEDSTEAD, with end poles, stuffed with horse hair in light blue silk damask, and curtains to correspond, lined with silk and silk fringe

793 The handsome gilt curtain cornices for two windows, and pins, 3 ft. 6 in.

794 The gilt cornice for bay window, *en suite*, 9 ft.

795 An inlaid mahogany chair with stuffed back and seat, Holland cover

796 A high back chair *en suite* covered in damask, Holland cover

797 A circular mahogany inlaid library chair, Holland cover

798 A mahogany frame couch, stuffed with horse hair in blue damask *en suite*, bolster and down pillow, Holland cover

799 An inlaid mahogany frame couch with circular end, Holland cover

800 A curious inlaid oval Pembroke table with drawer

801 A CAPITAL INLAID MAHOGANY WASHING STAND, with marble top, tray and cupboard, oval pole dressing glass, white and gold fittings, 2 covered water jugs, decanters, &c., &c.

802 A Queen's ware foot bath and large water jug

803 A mahogany bidet and pan

804 A mahogany tray top dressing table with two drawers

805 A swing dressing glass in mahogany frame, with two drawers

806 An inlaid mahogany flower table

807 A mahogany towel horse and boot jack

808 A mahogany tray top night commode

809 A mahogany frame dressing glass, with rising frame, pillar and claw

810 AN ANCIENT INLAID MARQUETRIE AND BUHL CABINET, with steel ornaments, plate glass panels

811 A HANDSOME TORTOISESHELL AND BUHL BRACKET CLOCK, with pillar front

No. 13, DRAWING ROOM.

812 AN ELEGANT ORMOLU AND POLISHED STEEL SCROLL FENDER, with ormolu standards and feet, and set of fire irons, with ormolu handles to correspond

813 A japanned vase-shaped coal receiver and brass wire guard

814 THE ELEGANT AXMINSTER TAPESTRY CARPET, about 80 square yards

815 The Holland covering over ditto, yards

816 Pieces of ditto to bay window

H

SEVENTH DAY'S SALE.

LOT

817 The Elegant Light Blue Silk Damask Curtains to Bay Windows, lined with silk, fringes, ropes and tassels, and rich gilt cornices

818 An Elegant Mahogany Chaise Lounge, in light blue satin damask, stuffed with horse hair, squab, bolster and down pillow, and holland cover

819 A ditto ditto *en suite*

820 A ditto Sofa, stuffed & covered *en suite*, with two down pillows & Holland cover

821 Six Elegant Chairs, with high backs, stuffed and covered *en suite*, and Holland covers

822 Six Elbow ditto *en suite*

823 A Pair of Bargiere ditto *en suite*

824 A pair of ditto *en suite*

825 A pair of cheval frame fire screens *en suite*

826 A pair of foot rests *en suite*

827 A pair of Ottoman stools *en suite*

828 A pair of blue sheepskin rugs

829 A Pair of Elegant inlaid Mahogany Pedestal Card Tables, lined with green cloth

830 A ditto chess table *en suite*

831 A ditto Circular Loo Table, 4 feet 3 diameter

832 A ditto Circular Card Table, with agate top and drawers

833 A ditto ditto

834 A Pair of Elegant Ormolu Tables, with marble top and claw feet, 2 feet 4 inches diameter

835 A Pair of Elegant Ormolu Candelabras for 12 Lights each on Sphinx Pedestals, and crimson silk covers

836 A pair of ditto ditto

837 A pair of ditto ditto

838 An Elegant Chandelier *en suite* for Twelve Lights.

839 A Richly carved gilt Pier Table on claw feet, with plate glass back and veined marble top

840 A noble Pier Glass in rich gilt frame, fine plate 96 by 60 inches

841 A ditto ditto

842 A carved mahogany wine cooler on pillar and claw pedestal, holland cover

843 An elegant carved Cabinet of Tulip wood, with four plate glass panels, mosaic marble top and moulding of verd antique

844 Sundries

845 Ditto

SEVENTH DAY'S SALE.

MUSICAL LIBRARY.

LOT

1 Kreutzer's Operas, P. F. and Violin.. 3 Vols.

2 Ditto, Mort D'Abel, 1; Castil Blaz, 3; Le Piccini and Collection (Operas) 5 ,,

3 De Lisle's Cinquante Chants Français and 48 Fugues and Preludes for P. F. by J. S. Bach ....

4 Fiovaranti Opera—I Virtuosi Ambulanti, 1; and Hummel's Concertos and Sonatas for P. F., 4 .... 5 ,,

5 Rossini's Siege de Corinth (in score).. 3 ,,

6 Paul et Virginie par Leseuer (in score) 1; Telemache, 1; and Crescentinis Exercises pour la Vocalisation Musicale, 1 .... 3 ,,

7 Collection of Operas, by Mozart, for P. F. .... 9 ,,

8 Ditto, 2; and Spohr's Collection for P. F., 1.. 3 ,,

9 Dalayrac's Operas, for P. F.. 6 ,,

10 Winter's Opera, Le Sacrifice, 1; Lachnite's Op. 1; Leseuer's Ossian, and Cherubini's Operas, for P.F.. 4 Books

11 Gluck's Iphigenie, 1; and Nicolo's Operas, 3, for P. F. .... 4 ,,

12 Spontini's Operas, 3; and Handel's Il Convito, 1, for P. F. .... 4 ,,

13 Beethoven's Op. Fidelio, 1; and Herold's Operas, 3, for P. F. .... 4 ,,

14 Mehul's Operas, for P. F.. 5 ,,

15 Pasiello's Opera; Nina, for P. F. and Voice, 1; Blangini's Nepthali, 1; Piscini, &c., 2; and Bochsa's Nocturnes, &c., for P. F. and Violin, 2 6 Books

16 Recueil, Music for Voice and P. F., by Paer, Pacini and Mercadante 4

17 Ditto, by Rossini, &c., 4; ditto by Martini, &c., 4.......................... 8 ,,

18 BEETHOVEN'S SONATAS for the P. F., *calf elegant* .... 2 Vols.

19 Ditto Trios, Quartuors, and Concertos, 1; and Variations, 1; for P. F. 2 Books

20 Rossini's Comte Ory, Opera in Two Acts, for Voice and P. F., *calf elegant;* and ditto L'Inganno Fortunato .... 2 ,,

21 MARCELLO'S PSALMS, *fine copy* .... 4 ,,

22 HAYDN'S SACRED MUSIC, Oratorios, Masses, &c., in score, (Porro) *calf*... 5 ,,

23 Haydn's Creation, (P. F. and Voices) 1; ditto Seasons, ditto, 1; ditto Seven Last Words, ditto, 1 .... 3 ,,

24 Righini's Mass for 4 Voices; Pergolese's Stabat Mater, 1; Chants, &c., de Sion, par Cæsar Malan, 1 .... 3 ,,

H 2

SEVENTH DAY'S SALE.

LOT		
25	BEETHOVEN'S Oratorio, Mount of Olives, (in score) *blue calf*, 1; Cimarosa's O Salutaris, (P. F. and 3 Voices)	2 Books
26	MOZART'S Requiem, in score; ditto Ave Verum, (P. F.)	3 „
27	HUMMEL, Parisot, Mozart, &c., in 1; Jomellis' Masses, &c., in score, 2	3 „
28	Fioravanti—Rigatti Durante, (Porro, Choran and Leo) ditto,	2 „
29	Cherubini—Requiem, in score, 1; ditto 12 Sacred Pieces, ditto, 2	3 „
30	HANDEL'S ORATORIOS, in score, (Walsh's edition):—Esther, Jeptha, Susannah, and Deborah, *calf*	4 Books
31	Ditto—The Resurrection, Samson, Semele, and Sosarme	4 „
32	Ditto—Agrippina, Theodora, and Israel in Egypt	4 „
33	Ditto—Alexander Balus, Judas Maccabæus, Saul, and Solomon	4 „
34	Ditto—Athalia, Alexander's Feast, Teseo, and Belshazzar	4 „
35	Ditto—Anthems	4 „
36	Ditto—The Triumph of Time and Truth, The Choice of Hercules, The Occasional Oratorio, Ode, and Alcides	4 „
37	Ditto—L'Allegro and Il Pensieroso, Sonatas, Duettos and Trios, Te Deum and Jubilate, and Te Deum and Concerto	5 „
38	Handel's Concertos	4 Vols.
39	Sundries	
40	Ditto	
41	Vogel—La Toison d'Or, Tragedie, in score	1 „
42	Mozart's Opera, Don Juan, in score, 1; and Cosi Fan tutti, 2	3 „
43	Mozart's Idomene	3 „
44	Ditto—Il Flauto Magico	2 „
45	Ditto—Il Nozze de Figaro	2 „
46	Ditto—Il ratto del Seraglio	2 .
47	Ditto—La Clemenza di Ti[illegible]	2 „
48	Mehul's Operas—Bayardo, Une Folie, and L'Irato	3 Books
49	Piccini's Operas—Didon	3 Vols.
50	Ditto—Roland, Atys, and Penelope	3 Books
51	Sacchini's Operas—Œdipus, and Dardanus	2 „
52	Boeldieu's Operas—La Petit Chaperon Rouge, Ma Tante Aurora, and La Dame Blanche, 3	5 Vols.
53	Ditto—La Calife de Bagdad, La Nouveau Seigneur, Jean de Paris, and Les Voitures Versées	4 Books
54	Ditto—Beniowski, Rien de Tout, La Jeune Femme Colèré, and Charles de France	4 „
55	Cherubini's Anacreon, Deux Journées, and Medée	4 „

SEVENTH DAY'S SALE.

LOT			
56	Salieri's Les Danaides, Paisiello's Proserpine, and La Forêt de Senart ...	4	Books
57	Nicolo's Operas—Une Jour à Paris, L'une pour L'autre, Le Médicin Turc, and Cendrillon	4	,,
58	Ditto—Lulli et Quinault, La Ruse Inutile, La Dejeuner, and Jeannot et Colin........	4	,,
59	Ditto—Cimarosa, Les Confidences, Joconde, and Rendezvous	4	,,
60	Ditto—La Française, Le Prince de Catane, La Magicienne, and Leonce	4	,,
61	Ditto Le Billet, Les Deux Maris, and Michael Ange	3	,,
62	CIMAROSA's Operas—Gli Orazi ej Curiazi, Matrimonio Segreto, and L'Impresario	5	,,
63	GLUCK's Operas—Alceste, Cythere Assigiè, and Orphée et Euridici	3	,,
64	Ditto, Iphigeni en Tauride, Echo et Narcisse, Armide, and Ephigeni en Aulide	4	,,
65	KREUTZER's Operas—Paul et Verginie, Aristippe, Lodoiska, and François I.	4	,,
66	Ditto—L'Homme sans Façon, Jadis et Anjour d'hui, and FIOVARANTI's I Virtuosi Ambulanti	4	,,
67	SPONTINI's Opera—La Vestale........	3	Vols.
68	Ditto—Ferdinand Cortez	3	,,
69	Ditto—Olimpé	3	,,
70	ROSSINI's Operas—Tancredi (P. F. and Voice), Ricciardo e Zoraide, and Zelmira........	3	Books
71	Ditto—Semiramide, Elizabeth, and Otello	3	,,
72	Ditto—Maometto Secondo, Armida, Il Turco in Italia, and La Donna del Lago	4	,,
73	Ditto—Corradino, La Cenerentola, and Mosè in Egitto	3	,,
74	Ditto, Inganno Felice, Il Barbier de Siviglia, Italiani in Algieri, and La Gazza Ladra	4	,,
75	WEBER's Opera Der Freischutz, and MEYERBEER's Il Crociato in Egitto..	[illegible]	,,
76	Paer's Operas—Le Maîitre de Chapelle, Agnese, Camilla, and Griselda	4	,,
77	AUBER's OPERAS, for P. F., &c.	6	,,
78	Mercadante's Eliza, 1; Cembalos, Eliza and Claudia, Boieldieu's La Dame Blanche, and Auber's La Neige........	4	,,
79	Boieldieu's Operas........	8	Vols.
80	Berton's Operas, 7; and ditto Canons, 1	8	,,
81	Catel's Operas (P. F. and Voice)	2	,,
82	GRETRY's Operas (in score)—Anacreon, Cephale et Procris, Colinette à la Cour, and La Caravane du Caire	4	,,
83	Ditto—Andromache, Panurge, L'Ami de la Maison, and Les Deux Avares	4	,,

SEVENTH DAY'S SALE.

LOT		
84	GRETRY'S L'Epreuve Villageois, L'Huron, L'Amitie Epreuve, and Zemire et Azor	
85	Ditto—Le Magnifique, Pierre le Grand, Le Mariage d'Anton, and Le Meprises	4 Vols.
86	Ditto—Le Raoul Barbe Bleue, Silvain, Judgment de Midas, & Guillaume Tell	4 „
87	Ditto—Elizabeth, L'Amant Jaloux, Rosière de Salenci, and Aucassin et Nicolette	4 „
88	Ditto—Les Evènements Impreuves, Elisca, Le Comte d'Albert, and Le Rival Confidant	4 „
89	Ditto—La Fausse Magie, Richard Cœur de Lion, Le Tableau Parlant, and Lucile	4 „
90	GRETRY'S Operas, P. F., 2; Le Moyne's Phædre, 1; and Catel's Les Artistes, 1	4 „
91	L. Persui's Jerusalem Deliverée, 3; and Phillidor's Opera Le Socier (in score), 1	3 Vols.
92	BERTON'S Operas—François de Foix, Valentin, Montano et Stephanie, and Romance	4 Books
93	Ditto—Le Vaisseau, La Grand Deuil, Les Deux Mousqetaires, and Les Maris Garçon	4 „
94	Ditto—Virginie, 3; Roger de Sicile, 1; and Aline, 1	5 „
95	DALAYRAC'S Operas (in score)—Koulouf, Marianna, Nina, and Ambroise	4 „
96	Ditto—Gulistan, L'Amant Statuè, Raoul, and La Soirée Oraguense	4 „
97	Ditto—Une Heure de Mariage, La Famille Americaine, Maison a Vendre, and Alexis	4 „
98	Ditto—Le Château, Le Pavillon, La Famille Americaine, and Philippe et Georgette	4 „
99	Ditto—Azemia, Lena, Une Matinè, and Camille & Sargines	5 „
100	La Maison Isolu, Les Deux Tuteurs, Ladot, and Adele et Dorsan	4 „
101	Ditto—La Leçon, Renaud, Les Deux Petits & Une Matinè, and La Bonde de Cheveux	5 „
102	AUBER'S Operas (in score)—Leicester, Fiorella, Concer à la Cour, Le Macon, and Leocæde	5 „
103	Ditto Le Timide, La Bergere, Emma, and La Neige	4 „
104	Winter's Opera Tamerlan; Felix Comedie, in Three Acts; Musique des Chansons de Beranger, *morocco gilt*	
105	Chants Populaires, 3, and Chansons et Airs du Bearn, *blue morocco gilt*	
106	Geiger's Masse Solennelle, *in velvet and silk binding*	

SEVENTH DAY'S SALE.

LOT

107 Encyclopédie Pittoresque de Musique, by Ledhuy and Berlini, Paris, 1834; and Orpheus Caledonices, by Thompson, 2.................. 3 Books

108 French Royal Chapel Music, Operas in MSS. ....24 Vols.

109 Ditto ditto ditto....................................24 „

110 Thirteen Volumes, various...13 „

111 Lully's Operas—Roland, Idylle, Persée, Thesée; Montclair's Jepthe, Circe .... 7 Books

112 Cantates, 1; Les Voyages, &c.; Blamont Clerembault, 2; Le Soleil, Léandre et Hero ....

113 Lully's Operas—Bellerophon, Proserpine, Orphée, Armide, Amadis, Charpentier's Medee.. 7 Books

114 Ditto—Telemaque, Isis, Atys, Arethuse, Hesoine, Tancrede, Amadis Phæton, Cadmus, *folio MSS*... 9 „

115 Motetts de Lalande (Royal Collection) .... 4 Vols.

116 Operas—L'Europe, Scylla, Les Amours, Marthesie, Theagine, Arianne, La Naissance, Psyche, Omphale, Les Jestes de l'Amour, Carnaval de Venise, Venus et Adonis, and Alceste (Royal MSS.)..............

117 Le Triomphe d'Amour, Achille et Polixene; Cantates, 2; Tancrede, and 8 other Operas ....

118 Cantates, &c., 28, various (*MSS.*)

119 Operas, &c., 23, various (*MSS.*)

120 Cantates Française, 5; Operas, &c., 28, various

121 Thirty Volumes of Ancient French Chamber Operas

122 Ditto ditto ditto

123 Ditte ditto ditto

124 Ditto ditto ditto

125 Forty-six ditto ditto

126 Hummel's Concertos, [illegible]6 parts; Giordani's ditto, [illegible] parts........

127 J. B. Cramer's Sonatas for P. F.; Mozart's Il Flauto Magico (P. F. and Voice), and 4 others...

128 Baudouin's Quadrilles, &c.; 2 other volumes of Modern Music; Beethoven's Temma, &c. (Violin and Violoncello); and Grand Trio ...

129 Mayseder Rovedino for P. F.; Garandi's Method; Le Soirée de Famille; and 2 others; and Beethoven's Quartett, &c., *unbound*, (*in folio*) ....

130 Don Giovanni as P. F. Duetts, ; Rossini's P. F. Duetts, 6; Latour's ditto, 2; Dussek's ditto, ;..

131 Rossini's Maometto, &c.; and a parcel of various Airs, *unbound*........

SEVENTH DAY'S SALE.

LOT	
132	Weber's Oberon for P. F. and Voice; Mozart's Sonata; Pergolesi's Stabat Mater; and a collection of Airs .. ..
133	La Muette de Portici, by Auber; and a parcel unbound..................
134	Reigir's Exercises, &c.; and a parcel unbound ....
135	J. B. Cramer's Studies, &c.; and a parcel unbound.........................
136	H. Herz, and other Music unbound ....
137	Kalkbrenner, &c., and a larger parcel unbound ....
138	Sundries ....
139	Ditto ....

End of Seventh Day's Sale.

EIGHTH DAY'S SALE,

AT RUSHTON HALL, NEAR KETTERING, NORTHAMPTONSHIRE,

On WEDNESDAY, 15th AUGUST, 1855,

Commencing at Eleven for Twelve o'Clock precisely.

CELLAR OF WINES.

SHERRY.

Bin No. 44.

LOT				
1	Two dozens of rich brown Sherry, (*Garcia's*) bottles included			at per dozen
2	Two dozens	ditto	ditto	"
3	Two dozens	ditto	ditto	"
4	Two dozens	ditto	ditto	"
5	Two dozens	ditto	ditto	"
6	Two dozens	ditto	ditto	"
7	Three dozens (more or less)	ditto	ditto	"

Bin No. 38.

LOT				
8	Two dozens of pale Sherry, (*Garcia's*) bottles included			"
9	Two dozens	ditto	ditto	"
10	Two dozens	ditto	ditto	"
11	Two dozens	ditto	ditto	"
12	Two dozens	ditto	ditto	"
13	Two dozens	ditto	ditto	"
14	Two dozens	ditto	ditto	"
15	Two dozens (more or less)	ditto	ditto	"
16	Sundries			
17	Ditto			

EIGHTH DAY'S SALE.

Bin No. 19.

LOT				
44	Two dozens *Rudesheimer*, 1811, A 20, bottles included			at per dozen
45	Two dozens	ditto	ditto	,,
46	Two dozens (more or less)	ditto	ditto	,,

Bin No. 32.

47	Two dozens Hock, *Mappes*, 1811, A 10—very superior—bottles included			,,
48	Two dozens	ditto	ditto	,,
49	Two dozens	ditto	ditto	,,
50	Two dozens	ditto	ditto	,,
51	Two dozens	ditto	ditto	,,
52	Two dozens	ditto	ditto	,,
53	Two dozens	ditto	ditto	,,
54	Two dozens	ditto	ditto	,,
55	Two dozens	ditto	ditto	,,
56	Two dozens	ditto	ditto	,,
57	Two dozens and a half	ditto (more or less)	ditto	,,
58	Sundries			
59	Ditto			

CLARET.

Bin No. 7.

60	Two dozens Claret St. Julien (from Cassey and Mauleon) very good, bottles included			,,
61	Two dozens	ditto	ditto	,,
62	Two dozens	ditto	ditto	,,
63	Two dozens	ditto (more or less)	ditto	,,

Bin No. 8.

64	Two dozens	ditto	ditto	,,
65	Two dozens	ditto	ditto	,,
66	Two dozens	ditto	ditto	,,
67	Two dozens	ditto	ditto	,,
68	Two dozens	ditto	ditto	,,
69	Two dozens	ditto	ditto	,,
70	Two dozens	ditto	ditto	,,

I 2

EIGHTH DAY'S SALE.

LOT				
71	Two dozens Claret St. Julien, (from Cassey & Mauleon), very good, bottles included			at per dozen.
72	Two dozens	ditto	ditto	"
73	Two dozens	ditto	ditto	"
74	Two dozens	ditto	ditto	"
75	Two dozens	ditto	ditto	"
76	Two dozens	ditto	ditto	"
77	Two dozens and a half	ditto	ditto	"

Bin No. 9.

78	Two dozens	ditto	ditto	"
79	Two dozens	ditto	ditto	"
80	Two dozens	ditto	ditto	"
81	Two dozens	ditto	ditto	"
82	Two dozens	ditto	ditto	"
83	Two dozens	ditto	ditto	"
84	Two dozens	ditto	ditto	"
85	Two dozens	ditto	ditto	"
86	Two dozens	ditto	ditto	"
87	Two dozens	ditto	ditto	"
88	Two dozens	ditto	ditto	"
89	Two dozens	ditto	ditto	"
90	One dozen and a half (more or less)		ditto	"

Bin No. 41.

91	Two dozens Claret. "La Rose" (*Begermann*, A 5) bottles included		
92	Two dozens	ditto	"
93	Three dozens (more or less)	ditto	"

Bin No. 40.

94 One dozen and nine "Chateau Margeaux" (*Begermann*, 1825, A 7), bottles included at per dozen.

Bin No. 41.

95	Two dozens of "Laffitte" Claret (*Begermann*, 1825, A 7), excellent—bottles included		at per dozen.
96	Two dozens ditto	ditto	"
97	Three dozens (more or less)	ditto	"

EIGHTH DAY'S SALE.

Bin No. 30.

LOT				
98	Two dozens Claret, "Hautbrion," very fine (*J. H. Begermann*, 1825), bottles included			at per dozen
99	Two dozens	ditto	ditto	,,
100	Two dozens	ditto	ditto	,,
101	One dozen and a half (more or less)	ditto	ditto	,,

Bin No. 29.

102	Fourteen bottles "Laffite" (*Wilson & Cutler*, 1825), bottles included	,,

Bin No. 26.

103	Two dozens "Chateau Margeaux" (*Wilson & Cutler*, 1825), bottles included			at per dozen
104	Two dozens	ditto	ditto	,,
105	Two dozens	ditto	ditto	,,
106	Two dozens	ditto	ditto	,,
107	Two dozens	ditto	ditto	,,
108	Two dozens	ditto	ditto	,,
109	Two dozens	ditto	ditto	,,
110	Two dozens	ditto	ditto	,,
111	Three dozens and four	ditto	ditto	,,

PORT.

Bin No. 50.

112	Two dozens of fine Port, bottles included			,,
113	Two dozens	ditto	ditto	,,
114	Three dozens (more or less)		ditto	

Bin No. 51.

115	Two dozens fine Port, bottles included			,,
116	Two dozens	ditto	ditto	,,
117	Two dozens	ditto	ditto	,,
118	Two dozens	ditto	ditto	,,
119	Two dozens (more or less)		ditto	,,

Bin No. 52.

120	Three dozens old Port, bottles included	,,

EIGHTH DAY'S SALE.

VARIOUS.

Bin No. 53.

LOT		
121	Two dozen pints of dry Lachrymosa, bottles included	”
122	One dozen and three pints Muscat Reveiro, ditto	”
123	One dozen and three quarts Vagariam ditto	”
124	One dozen and three quarts Priora Macabeo, ditto	”
125	Two dozen quarts Muscat Wyn ditto	”
126	Twelve bottles Beste Geneva (*Het Leolsie*)	
127	Eight bottles Curaçoa and nine Anisette	
128	Sundries	
129	Ditto	
130	Ditto	
131	Ditto	
132	Ditto	

FOWLING PIECES, &c.

133	A single barrelled Fowling Piece, by *Manton*	
134	A ditto by *Jackson*, with case, &c.	
135	A ditto ditto	
136	An excellent double barrelled Fowling Piece, by *Jackson*, with case and fittings	
137	A valuable Rifle, by *Gosset*, with mahogany case and fittings	
138	An excellent double barrelled Fowling Piece, by *Westley Richards*, with mahogany case and fittings, and extra leather travelling case	
139	A ditto ditto	
140	A brace of pistols, powder horn, and case (at Bailiff's)	
141	Two muskets with bayonets	
142	Two ditto	
143	Two ditto	
144	Two ditto	
145	Two ditto	
146	Two ditto (at Bailiff's)	
147	Two ditto	

EIGHTH DAY'S SALE.

LOT
148 Two muskets with bayonets (at Bailiff's)
149 A Court Dress Sword and Clasp, by *Gray*, of Sackville Street
150 A strait sword with brass handle and steel sheath
151 A ditto, steel handle
152 A cavalry sword and sheath
153 A wainscot case with fishing rods and tackle
154 Fishing rods and tackle, various
155 A pair of Swans
156 One ditto
157 A Pleasure Boat with oars
158 A fishing Punt
158* A casting Net
159 A ditto
159* A sean Net with corks and leads
160 A large Drag Net with ditto
161 A quantity of Game Nets (in Bailiff's house)
162 A quantity of ditto ditto

GARDENS.

163 A 1-light Melon Frame
164 A 2-light ditto
165 A ditto ditto
166 A ditto ditto
167 A 3-light ditto
168 A ditto ditto
169 Six hand lights
170 Six ditto
171 Six ditto
172 Six ditto
173 A 12-step ladder and two watering pots
174 A wheelbarrow and two watering pots
175 Ditto and ditto
176 Three watering pots, two circular bell glasses, and sundry netting
177 An iron balance weight garden roller
178 A quantity of zinc wire netting
179 Various garden tools

John Cruikshank, and family outside their cottage in the hall grounds.

Rushton Hall kitchen gardens, greenhouses, and visitors.

EIGHTH DAY'S SALE.

LOT
180 Various garden tools
181 A large green painted garden seat
182 A ditto
183 Two smaller ditto
184 Two ditto
185 Two ditto

GREENHOUSE.

186 Fifty Greenhouse Plants in pots
187 Fifty ditto
188 Fifty ditto
189 Fifty ditto
190 Fifty ditto
191 Fifty ditto
192 Fifty ditto
193 Fifty ditto
194 A quantity of garden pots and sundries

End of Eighth Day's Sale.

Inside the greenhouse at Rushton Hall with Head Gardener John Cruikshank on the right

Grapes in the greenhouse, the only variety of grape grown at the Hall was `The Black Hambro`.

NINTH DAY'S SALE,

AT RUSHTON HALL, NEAR KETTERING, NORTHAMPTONSHIRE,

ON THURSDAY, 16TH AUGUST, 1855,

Commencing at Eleven for Twelve precisely.

No. 37, LINEN ROOM.

LOT

846 A brass mounted fender and fire irons, and wire guard

847 Two plate boxes and a mahogany towel horse

848 Two cases of minerals and twelve green lamp shades and frames

849 A stout deal table

850 A ditto

851 A capital large stout laundry table, with six drawers and folding doors under, 9 feet 6 long by 3 feet 9 wide

852 A mahogany arm-chair, stuffed with horse hair, covered with leather

853 A pair of painted double steps, two caned seat chairs, coal hod, and stool

854 A large black marble slab, feet by

855 Two pair of scarlet moreen window curtains trimmed, and bed furniture to match

856 Ditto and ditto

857 Ditto and ditto

858 Pair of scarlet damask window curtains (unmade), and a set of green damask window curtains fringed

859 A pair of crimson ditto, a pair of short curtains, several pieces of canvas, three pieces of calico, a quantity of fringe, and a quantity of brass curtain bands, rings, and brass work

860 A cloth table cover, holland ditto, an urn rug, and a quantity of blind cording and worsted cord

861 A pair of bronze candlesticks, and a bronze gothic night lamp and pair of snuffers and stand (No. 37)

862 A pair of ormolu ditto, & a bronze gothic night lamp & pair of snuffers & stand

863 Two pair of blue China high candlesticks and pair of snuffers (37)

864 Two pair of brown China ditto and pair of snuffers

865 Two pair of smaller ditto and three flat ditto

866 Three pair of ditto and three flat ditto

K

NINTH DAY'S SALE.

LOT
867 Four pair of ditto
868 Two pair of snuffers and stand, two pair of brooms, and a pair of bellows
869 Ditto ditto
870 A pair of papier maché bellows, 2 pairs of others ditto, and 2 hearth brooms

No. 3, FRONT ROOM ADJOINING.

871 A brass fender, fire irons, and guard, and a japanned coal receiver and cover
872 A Scotch carpet about 20 yards, a piece of oil cloth, and a boot jack
873 A Spanish mahogany French bedstead, green damask hangings
874 A straw palliasse and a wool mattress in tick
875 A wool bed
876 A ditto and feather bolster
877 Three blankets, a sheet, and white coverlid
878 An Easy chair stuffed with hair, cushion, and chintz cover
879 A mahogany tray top pot cupboard and five japanned gothic chairs
880 A mahogany bidet and pan, and towel horse
881 A mahogany pedestal table
882 A japanned washstand and fittings
883 A ditto dressing table and a mahogany framed swing dressing glass

No. 4. STORE ROOM.

884 A gothic brass lamp
885 Thirty-six brass stair rods and three brass ornaments
886 A hall stove with pipe and pan
887 A brass mounted fender and two brass fire guards
888 Three pieces of Brussels carpet and a sheep skin rug
889 A handsome crimson bordered Brussels stair carpet, about 26 yards
890 Forty brass stair rods
891 A Brussels rug, a piece of carpet and of drugget, and a rope mat

NINTH DAY'S SALE.

No. 10, BACK BED CHAMBER, ADJOINING.

LOT

892 An iron fender with standards, set of fire irons, and brass wire guard
893 An elegant flowered pattern Tapestry Carpet, about 30 yards
894 A hearth rug to match and a mahogany towel horse
895 A ditto, and ditto, and a boot jack
896 Three blankets (37)
897 Two pairs of ditto
898 A feather bolster and two down pillows
899 Ditto and ditto
900 A feather bolster, 2 feather pillows, and 1 down ditto
901 Three feather bolsters and 1 horse hair ditto
902 Two feather bolsters and 4 pillows (4)
903 An embroidered muslin bed covering
904 Six chair cushions stuffed with horse hair
905 A mahogany inlaid Couch stuffed with hair, squab, bolster and down pillow, in chintz *ensuite*, and cotton cover to ditto
906 Pair of curtains and valens *ensuite*, brass cornice pole and rings gilt ends
907 A mahogany inlaid Easy chair *ensuite*, in chintz and extra cover
908 A mahogany washstand with marble top, 2 drawers, blue and white fittings
909 A mahogany tray top dressing table, 3 drawers
910 A mahogany bidet and pan, and a Queen's ware foot bath and jug
911 A mahogany Pedestal Library Table with drawer, green cloth top
912 A mahogany Cabinet, inlaid with satinwood *ensuite*, folding doors and veined marble top
913 Three mahogany carved framed chairs *ensuite*, with Holland covers, and a lyre-shaped swing dressing glass, mahogany frame
914 A chimney glass in gilt frame, plate 54 by 44 inches
915 A French clock with bronze figure ornaments and glass shade
916 The crimson Brussels carpet to landing and part of No. 10 Room, about yards
917 The Holland carpet covering

No. 11, HALL ROOM.

918 An iron fender with set of fire irons, and a japanned Sarcophagus coal receiver with cover
919 An oil cloth to room, about 6 yards by 5 yards

K 2

NINTH DAY'S SALE.

LOT

920 A rosewood Sofa Table on pillar claw, with 2 drawers, and oil skin cover

921 A carved rosewood frame Elbow chair, in red leather, stuffed with horse hair, loose squab, extra Holland cover

922 A ditto ditto

923 Six carved mahogany pillar framed chairs, with loose seats stuffed with hair in scarlet leather

924 Six ditto ditto

925 A large circular Hall Lamp, brass frame and chain

926 A small ditto, bronze frame and chain

927 A HANDSOME TORTOISESHELL AND EBONY CABINET, with numerous drawers, ornaments, &c., on twisted pillars

No. 12, GUN ROOM.

928 A brass mounted fender, fire irons, guard, and 4 chairs

929 A wainscot table with drawer, a stout form, a stool, and iron frame camp stool

930 An inlaid mahogany Winged Bookcase, witth secretary, cupboard under, and 8 drawers

931 The oil cloth in passage, about 24 yards

932 Ditto ditto about 30 yards

933 A wainscot hat stand with branches

CHINA SERVICES.

934 AN ELEGANT WHITE, DRAB, AND GOLD DINNER SERVICE, viz., 2 soup tureens, covers and stands, 19 dishes in sizes, 6 vegetable dishes and covers, 6 sauce tureens, 2 cheese stands, fish drainer. and 120 plates

935 A DESSERT SERVICE *en suite*, viz., centre and 9 dishes

936 A TEA AND COFFEE SERVICE *en suite*

937 AN ELEGANT PINK AND GOLD DINNER SERVICE, viz., 3 soup tureens, covers and stands, 29 vegetable and other covered dishes, 9 sauce tureens, covers and stands, 1 cheese stand, 21 dishes in sizes, 4 pie ditto, 2 cheese stands, 3 fish drainers, and 240 plates

938 A DESSERT SERVICE *en suite*, with 11 dishes

939 A DINNER SERVICE OF GREEN, WHITE, AND GOLD, viz., 8 vegetable dishes and covers, 3 sauce tureens, covers and stands, 6 dishes in sizes, and 75 plates

940 A breakfast service *en suite*

NINTH DAY'S SALE.

LOT

941 A breakfast, tea and coffee service

942 A ditto dessert service, 117 pieces

943 A Tea and Coffee service of olive, drab, and gold, 60 pieces

944 A set of varied pattern cups and saucers, 50 pieces

945 Four white and gold dishes, and a tray with white and gold coffee china, 8 pieces

946 A HANDSOME CIRCULAR CHINA ROSE-WATER DISH, 22 inches diameter

947 A pair of wedgwood wine coolers and 6 chamber candlesticks

948 A pair of tureens, salad bowl, cheese stand, and 12 dishes

949 A bronze tea urn, with plated tap

CUT GLASS.

950 A pair of elegant cut Quart Decanters with stoppers

951 Two pair of ditto

952 Two pair of ditto and 2 pair of pint ditto

953 Ditto ditto

954 Three cut water jugs

955 A plain ditto and 4 cut jars with covers

956 Two cut water jugs and 14 cut wine glasses

957 Two cut water jugs and 14 plain wine glasses

958 Two dozen globe-shaped ditto

959 Eleven cut champagne glasses and 14 claret ditto

960 Twenty plain champagne ditto

961 Twenty-four claret ditto and 20 green hock ditto

962 One dozen cut rummers

963 Eighteen ditto

964 Fourteen water carafts and tumblers

965 Four soda-water glasses, 2 high rummers, and 9 plain finger glasses

966 Thirteen cut finger glasses and 24 jelly glasses

967 Twenty-six plain ditto and 22 ditto

968 Twenty-six cut finger glasses with drinking ditto

969 A cut water decanter and tumbler, 5 blue finger glasses, and 18 cut sweetmeat stands

970 Twenty-four cut sweetmeat stands

971 A cut trifle dish, a ditto butter dish, cover and stand, and a sugar glass

972 A pair of cut butter glasses, covers and stands, a sugar ditto and stand, and cut fruit dishes

NINTH DAY'S SALE.

LOT

973 An effervescing apparatus
974 A ditto
975 Two bronze inkstands with two glasses each (37)
976 Two black japanned ditto, with single glasses each, and 2 cast ditto with 2 glasses
977 A tortoiseshell ditto, with two glasses, and Barclay's night lamp
978 Six hearth brooms
979 Six ditto
980 Four ditto

LINEN.

981 Three pair of fine linen sheets—No. 6
982 Three pair ditto
983 Three pair ditto
984 Three pair ditto
985 Three pair ditto
986 Three pair ditto
987 Three pair ditto
988 Two large damask table cloths—No. 9
989 Two ditto
990 Two ditto
991 Three ditto
992 Five smaller ditto
993 Two large damask ditto (new), 4½ yards long—No. 10.
994 Three ditto, ditto
995 Four ditto, 2½ yards long
996 Two dozen table napkins
997 Three dozen ditto
998 Forty-two ditto—No. 8
999 Two dozen huckaback towels—No. 9
1000 Three dozen ditto
1001 Fourteen jack towels (No. 9), and 2 dozen glass cloths (No. 10)
1002 Thirty-eight knife cloths
1003 Forty cook's linen aprons
1004 Two dozen footman's new aprons
1005 Three dozen kitchen cloths, various

NINTH DAY'S SALE.

LOT
1006 Three dozen kitchen cloths, various
1007 Two dozen ditto
1008 Thirteen huckaback towels, 27 glass cloths, and 6 dusters
1009 Three dozen kitchen cloths, various
1010 Three dozen ditto
1011 Three dozen ditto
1012 Three dozen ditto

No. 18, KITCHEN.

1013 A slab iron fender and set of large fire irons
1014 A stout deal framed table with 4 drawers, 10 feet long
1015 A pair of steps and stool and stout chopping block
1016 A CAPITAL PAINTED MEAT SCREEN AND HOT CLOSET, LINED WITH TIN, IRON BAR, SHELVES, &c.
1016* A large brass framed circular suspending lamp with shade, 24 inches diameter
1017 An eight day dial in mahogany case, by *Whiteaves, Fleet Street*

FRENCH COOKING UTENSILS, &c.

1018 A copper dripping pan, iron stand, and ladle
1019 A ditto boiler with tap
1020 Seven ditto with lids
1021 A ditto fish kettle and a brazing kettle
1022 A ditto and ditto
1023 A ditto and ditto
1024 One larger ditto and 2 smaller ditto
1025 Two oval copper saucepans
1026 Six ditto saucepans in sizes, with lids
1027 Six ditto ditto
1028 Nine ditto ditto
1029 Twelve smaller ditto
1030 Twelve ditto
1031 Fifteen ditto
1032 Eight shallow copper pans
1033 Eight ditto

The old kitchen at Rushton Hall

Bailiffs House in the hall grounds

NINTH DAY'S SALE.

LOT

1034 Twelve copper saucepans with lids tinned

1035 Thirteen ditto

1036 Three ditto strainers, 3 ladles, and 7 ditto pudding moulds

1037 Fifteen ditto baking dishes

1038 Four copper lipped handle

1039 Four ditto stewpans

1040 Thirteen ditto baking trays

1041 One ditto preserving pan and 24 ditto spoons and forks, tinned

1042 Four tin dish covers, 1 tin dripping pan and ladle, a gridiron, a chopper, and sundry small tin ware

1043 A gridiron, a chopper, 8 confectionery tins, 18 iron skewers and forks, five choppers, and 30 wooden spoons

1044 A gridiron, four strainers, 16 wooden sieves, a chopper, and 12 fruit bottles

1045 Two marble pestles, three pastry boards and wood mortar, and two chopping boards

1046 A stout deal table with two drawers, 8 feet

1047 Two wooden stools, 2 chairs, 6 pastry boards, 2 Wedgwood butter pans

1048 A pair of oven tongs, shovel and sifter

1049 A copper fish kettle and steamer, and a preserving pan

1050 A copper mould and sundry tin moulds and copper wine muller

1051 A tin steamer with saucepan and preserving pan

1052 A ditto and ditto

1053 Six copper stewpans

1054 A ditto steamer and strainer, a ditto saucepan and a ladle

1055 Six ditto stewpans

1056 Twenty copper jelly moulds

1057 Two large ditto steamers, with covers and strainers

1058 Three large ditto saucepans

1059 A japanned plate warmer, a coffee mill with block and fly wheel, and sundry tin ware

1060 A copper brazing kettle (tinned) and 12 jelly moulds—No. 46

1061 A ditto and 13 jelly moulds

1062 Eight metal moulds

1063 Four dairy pails, a coffee pot, and tea kettle

1064 Three large copper saucepans, lipped

1065 Six ditto

1066 Six ditto

NINTH DAY'S SALE.

LOT

1067 Two slices, a straining spoon, a brazier bowl, and 2 pewter pots

1068 A large copper preserving pan

1069 A ditto

1070 Sundry tin pastry cutters, 5 tin baking dishes, and 2 pair of cooking tongs

1071 Four tin dish covers, 3 gauze meat ditto, 4 plate baskets, and 14 wood and iron spoons

PANTRY.

1072 A deal table (6 feet)

1073 A stout chopping block, one pickling tub and cover, iron cleaver and saw

BAKERY.

1074 A stout table with two drawers and two wood boxes

End of Ninth Day's Sale.

TENTH DAY'S SALE,

AT RUSHTON HALL, NEAR KETTERING, NORTHAMPTONSHIRE,

ON FRIDAY, THE 17TH OF AUGUST, 1855,

Commencing at Eleven for Twelve o'Clock precisely.

BAILIFF'S HOUSE, IN PARK,

(MR. WATKINSON'S.)

RIGHT HAND FRONT BED ROOM.

LOT

1075 A brass mounted fender and fire-irons
1076 A four-post bedstead, carved mahogany feet pillars
1077 A palliasse
1078 A wool mattress
1079 A feather bed and three bolsters
1080 A feather bed
1081 Nine matted chairs and one arm ditto, covered seat
1082 A mahogany tray top commode
1083 A corner washstand and fittings
1084 Curtains, cornices, and blinds

BEST BED ROOM.

1085 A brass mounted fender and a hearth rug
1086 A Scotch carpet to room, yards
1087 A 4-post bedstead, with carved feet, pillars, and chintz furniture
1088 A palliasse
1089 A wool mattress
1090 A feather bed, bolster, and two pillows
1091 A mahogany chest of five drawers
1092 An easy chair, with cushion, stuffed with hair in cotton
1093 Four matted chairs and one arm ditto, cane seat
1094 A japanned washstand, blue fittings, and a japanned dressing table, 2 drawers
1095 A ditto tray top ditto, and a swing dressing glass, in mahogany frame

TENTH DAY'S SALE.

LOT

1096 A large japanned washstand and a stool
1097 A mahogany bidet, and four matted chairs
1098 Two pair of crimson cloth window curtains, brass poles and bands
1099 Set of mahogany bed steps, and a green painted table
1100 A white painted press and a mahogany towel horse
1101 Sundries
1102 Ditto

BED ROOM ADJOINING.

1103 Curtain pole and rings, brass fittings
1104 A brass fender, a mahogany bidet, and a piece of Kidderminster carpet
1105 An iron bedstead
1106 A hair mattress
1107 A wool ditto
1108 A mahogany commode
1109 A large easy chair covered with cotton

BACK ROOM.

1110 A brass top fender, a deal box, and two tressels

KITCHEN.

1111 A fender and set of fire irons, and a hearth rug
1112 A stout deal table, three drawers, 7 feet long
1113 A ditto, 4 feet
1114 A wainscot Pembroke table with drawer
1115 A meat screen lined with tin
1116 A japanned plate warmer, a small wainscot table, four chairs, & one arm ditto
1117 Two cradle spits, a tin cheese toaster, a ditto tea pot, a candlestick, & sundries
1118 A copper warming pan and a pair of steelyards
1119 Sundry blue and white ware
1120 Two tea trays, knife box, spice box, and two chair back screens

L 2

TENTH DAY'S SALE.

BREWHOUSE.

LOT

1121 A five feet deal table with two drawers

1122 A flour tub, iron frying pan, chopper, saw, and sundries

PARLOUR.

1123 A steel fender, set of fire irons, a guard, and a hearth rug

1124 A Brussels carpet yards

1125 Six good mahogany chairs

1126 A rosewood sofa, covered with chintz, stuffed with horse-hair

1127 A set of mahogany dining tables, circular ends and shifting flaps, 10 feet by 4 feet 6 inches

1128 A mahogany Pembroke table, with drawer on pillar and claw

1129 Two japanned cane back arm chairs and cushions

1130 A pier glass, in gilt frame, plate 40 inches by 18

1131 A neat painted cheffonier

1132 Two pair of cotton window curtains and cornice

1133 A needlework portrait, two views of mansion, two portraits, a coloured print, and a plan

1134 Two mahogany hall chairs

1135 Two ditto

1136 A ditto table with two drawers

1137 A wainscot kneehole writing table with three drawers

OFFICE.

1138 A brass mounted fender, the oil cloth to office, and chairs

1139 Deal desk and stand with two drawers

1140 An office stool and footstool, a nest of boot and shoe shelves, and a small wainscot table

1141 A mahogany Pedestal Sideboard, with cellaret and plate drawers, 5 feet wide

1142 A three-fold clothes horse, a pair of steps, and a mahogany butler's tray and stand

1143 Sundries

1144 Ditto

TENTH DAY'S SALE.

CARPENTER'S SHOP.

LOT

1145 Four large picture frames
1146 Two large cupboards
1147 Long pair of steps and large wood basket
1148 Twelve door frames
1149 Six sashes and frames
1150 Four ditto
1151 Ten pair new ditto, various sizes
1152 Ten pair ditto
1153 Ten pair ditto
1154 Eight old doors and sashes
1155 Four new ditto
1156 Three ditto
1157 A cistern lined with lead
1158 A ditto ditto
1159 Four iron hopper heads
1160 Six lengths of iron pipe, sixteen iron gutters, and five elbow ditto
1161 Four packing cases, sundry boarding, &c.
1162 A muller, slab, and about one cwt. of white lead
1163 Sundry paint, cans, and pots
1164 Folding steps, and two tressels
1165 A roll of milled lead, about cwt.
1166 A piece of wire work
1167 Sundries
1168 Ditto
1169 A dog box and two pair of large hook and eye hinges
1170 One and a half pair of diagonal Gates, 15 feet high
1171 A stout framed bench with two drawers
1172 Two crates with sheet glass, and sundry glass in cupboard
1173 A crate of sheet glass
1174 A large packing case, two iron-bound boxes, and chain

CARPENTER'S SHOP IN LOFT.

1175 A carpenter's bench with screw
1176 A ditto

TENTH DAY'S SALE.

LOT

1177 A carpenter's bench and screw
1178 Half a load of lathes
1179 Four door frames
1180 Six new ledge doors
1181 Seven ditto and one ditto with lock
1182 Two pieces of mahogany
1183 Four new four-panel doors
1184 Five ditto
1185 Five ditto
1186 Seven ditto
1187 A pair of ledge gates, 8 feet opening
1188 A pair of gothic doors, 10 feet high by 6 feet wide
1189 Eleven new door frames
1190 About 300 feet of moulding
1191 Four frames with strained calico and two doors circular top
1192 Quantity of panelling
1193 About 2 cwt. of stout iron wire
1194 Ten hen coops
1195 A chopping block
1196 A glazed sash
1197 Sundries
1198 Ditto
1199 Ditto
1200 Ditto

CARRIAGE YARD, &c.

1201 A Carriage Break, with pole, &c.
1202 A Dog Cart in good condition
1203 A stout framed Luggage Cart
1204 A pair horse Harness
1205 A single horse ditto
1206 A saddle and bridle
1207 Ditto and ditto
1208 Ditto and ditto
1209 Sundry nag harness, bits, &c.

TENTH DAY'S SALE.

MARES, COLTS, &c.

LOT			
1210	A WELL BRED ROAN MARE, AND FOAL, BY MAROTTO (the Duke of Buccleugh's)		
1211	A 4-year old Bay Nag Filly, by METEOR		
1212	A 4-year old Bay Filly, by JOHNNY, from a half bred ARABIAN MARE		
1213	A 3-year old Bay Colt, by JOHNNY		
1214	A 2-year old Bay Colt, by MAROTTO		
1215	A Bay yearling Colt, by MAROTTO		
1216	A Roan ditto		
1217	A light chestnut ditto		
1218	A useful nag horse		
1219	Sundries		
1220	Ditto		

CART HORSES, &c.

1221	A powerful black Cart Horse, 7 years old,		*Captain*
1222	A grey ditto	ditto	*Trowler*
1223	A ditto	ditto	*Prince*
1224	A ditto	ditto	*Boxer*
1225	A Flemish Mare, *Margaret*		
1226	A two-year old black Cart Colt		
1227	A roan yearling ditto		
1228	A handsome Short-horn Milch Cow		
1229	A ditto ditto		
1230	A ditto ditto		
1231	A ditto ditto		
1232	A ditto ditto		
1233	A ditto ditto		
1234	A ditto ditto		
1235	A ditto ditto		
1236	A ditto ditto		
1237	Five fat Leicester Lambs		
1238	Five ditto ditto		
1239	Five ditto ditto		
1240	Five ditto ditto		

TENTH DAY'S SALE.

LOT	
1241	Five fat Leicester Lambs
1242	Five ditto ditto
1243	Five ditto ditto
1244	Five ditto ditto
1245	Five fat Leicester Sheep, marked
1246	Five ditto ditto
1247	Five ditto ditto
1248	Five ditto ditto
1249	Five ditto ditto
1250	Five ditto ditto
1251	Sundries
1252	Ditto
1253	A Breeding Sow
1254	Two Porkers
1255	Two ditto
1256	Two ditto
1257	Two ditto
1258	Three ditto
1259	Sundry Poultry
1260	Sundries

GARDENER'S COTTAGE.

1261	Six chairs
1262	A bedstead, &c.

WAGGONS, HARNESS, &c.

1263	A good Broad-wheel Waggon
1264	A ditto
1265	A Timber Carriage
1266	A capital Wood Roller, iron bound
1267	A smaller ditto
1268	A pair of harrows
1269	A pair of ditto

TENTH DAY'S SALE.

LOT
1270 An iron *Ball's* plough
1271 A ditto
1272 Sundries
1273 Ditto
1274 A set of cart harness
1275 A set of ditto
1276 Ditto
1277 Ditto
1278 Ditto
1279 Ditto

RICK YARD.

1280 A dressing machine
1281 Six feet iron hurdles
1282 Felled oak trees
1283 Ditto
1284 Ditto
1285 Ditto, and saplings
1286 Ditto and ditto
1287 A quantity of charcoal (about cwt.)
1288 Sundries
1289 A Rick of Beans (about 15 quarters)
1290 A Rick of Peas (about 6 quarters)
1291 A Rick Cloth and two sets of tackling to ditto
1292 Sundries
1293
1294
1295

THE END.

Thompson and Vincent, Printers, 19, Great St. Helen's Bishopsgate.

M

Rushton Hall 2006

Today's East façade little changed since the days of W.W. Hope.

The court yard always a peaceful haven.

Rushton Hall Hotel

Today Rushton Hall is a grand hotel, resplendent with it's historical fireplaces still in situe retaining the heart of the building, the Grand hall, a very comfortable lounge in which to take coffee or an aperitif before moving past the library to the dining room. Upstairs, has been extensively modernised and tastefully refitted as bedroom suites.

The Great Hall, at Rushton Hall Hotel back in full splendour as today's hotel lounge.

This book was produced and published by Mr. David Palmer

Printed by Phoenix Printing Company.